BUILDING
COMMUNITIES
of LEARNERS

BUILDING COMMUNITIES of LEARNERS

A Collaboration among Teachers, Students, Families, and Community

Sudia Paloma McCaleb

New College of California

St. Martin's Press, New York

Editor: Naomi Silverman
Managing editor: Patricia Mansfield-Phelan
Project editor: Diana Puglisi
Production supervisor: Alan Fischer
Art director: Sheree Goodman
Cover and text design: Eileen Burke
Cover art: Deborah Green

Library of Congress Catalog Card Number: 92-62800

8 7 6 5 4
f e d c b a

For information, write:
St. Martin's Press, Inc.
175 Fifth Avenue
New York, NY 10010

ISBN: 0-312-09163-X

30003787

Acknowledgments

"Ya Gotta Know Somethin' 'Bout History" written by Kerrigan Black © 1990 Heebie
Jeebie Music, BMI, all rights reserved.

Dedicated to all children and their families
who enter schools with open eyes, minds, and hearts
seeking learning, nourishment, and validation
—and to their teachers who will welcome them.

FOREWORD

Children live their lives in two worlds: that of the home and community and that of the school. When these two worlds fail to know, respect, and celebrate each other, children are placed in a difficult position. Upon going to school, children from homes where the language is other than English, from homes struggling with poverty, or from cultures or ethnicity unlike those who hold power in this country frequently face the devaluing of their own reality and the disenfranchising of their own parents or primary caretakers.

The lack of ongoing contact between the school and the home and of an authentic incorporation of the child's reality into the curriculum perpetuates the idea that parents cannot contribute to their own children's education. As students discover the tremendous discrepancy between what the school proposes as accepted models and their own life experiences, profound inner conflicts develop. Since our society tends to view reality with a binary focus, dichotomizing between good and bad, acceptable and unacceptable, children exposed to the undeclared conflict between their two worlds feel compelled to make painful decisions about their families, their communities, their schools, and their own identities. Instead of being a secure haven for children's development, schools can be seriously detrimental to their growth.

Students easily understand (although they are seldom able to consciously verbalize it) when the curriculum and pedagogical practices do not fully respect their home culture and do not incorporate their parents and family. Weak efforts to pay lip service to pluralism succeed only in momentarily obscuring the issue. Nonetheless, the effects are deeply felt. The school's failure to acknowledge and value the family's learning and knowledge has a detrimental effect not only on the children's image of their parents but also on the students' appreciation of themselves as members of their home culture.

In *Building Communities of Learners*, Sudia Paloma McCaleb presents a powerful analysis of the dangers inherent to traditional schooling processes and examines some compelling alternative possibilities. Drawing not only from scholarly research and model experiences of progressive parent involvement programs throughout the country, but also from her own ample experience as educator and activist, McCaleb describes the challenge and encourages her readers to engage in a critical personal reflection that will allow them to generate creative responses and liberatory practices. Moreover, inspired by the philosophy of participatory research, Sudia Paloma McCaleb enriches her book with the significant voices of children and their parents.

Too much of what is attempted in education is done *to* students and their parents rather than *with* them. As a result, even some very well-intended efforts continue to perpetuate the notion that the capacity to know and to generate new knowledge is a privilege of some, rather than a birthright of every individual, ontologically inherent to every human being. Thus, it is refreshing, as well as a source of hope and inspiration, to center a book on the words of children and their parents. In this book, stories and reflections are shared and dreams and hopes revealed as an invitation to educators to recognize that, while much work remains to be done, schools can become truly democratic spheres for human growth, if we recognize the innate potential in all human beings for the construction of an equitable, just, and responsible social reality.

Alma Flor Ada
University of San Francisco

PREFACE

In the past two decades, political and economic dislocations around the world have stimulated a surge of immigration to the shores of the United States. In virtually every city in the country, we find new arrivals from a multitude of ethnic, national, cultural, and language groups. Immigrants bring with them their dreams and aspirations for success in a new land. At the same time, they find themselves struggling to understand a new culture, and it is not uncommon for them to encounter prejudice and racism. These new immigrants may be unable to speak English and are often without the skills or the benefit of a formal education from their homeland. This places an enormous burden on the shoulders of the young students who find themselves caught between two cultures.

The children of new immigrants make up a growing percentage of students in U.S. public schools today. The 1990 national census found that in the total school-age population, one in seven students speaks a language other than English at home. Three-quarters of these students live in households where everyone speaks the non-English language. Between 1980 and 1990 there was an estimated 38 percent increase in the numbers of home speakers of non-English languages aged five or older.

Across the country, teachers are challenged to teach this diverse population of students, who bring to school a wide variety of cultural practices and are dealing with the difficulties of adjusting to a new culture, a new educational system, and in many cases a new language.

Today's educators also face a tremendous opportunity to appreciate the rich and diverse ways in which language is used in the home and within the family and community, and to help their students to do the same. My contention, supported by the research cited in the present volume, is that this challenge of educating all students can be met only by addressing the central question posed in *Building Communities of Learners*:

How can educators create a partnership with parents and young students that will nurture literacy and facilitate participation in the schools while celebrating and validating the home culture and family and community concerns and aspirations?

THE MOTIVATION FOR THIS BOOK

This book grew out of my own experience during twenty years of teaching in diverse classrooms, involvement in community-based cultural organizations, and recent participatory research for my doctoral dissertation.

As I began to write, my thoughts frequently returned to Lilly, a student whom I supervised during her preservice work. After obtaining her bilingual accreditation, she was offered an emergency teaching position in a second-grade class composed of twenty-seven Spanish- and four English-speaking students. The opportunity arose because the regular classroom teacher was taking an unexpected leave four months before the end of the school year. After Lilly enthusiastically accepted the new job, she asked my advice: "Where and how will I begin?" Such a simple question!

My response was also simple and what I considered logical:

I would write a letter home to the families of the students, introducing myself and inviting them all to tea. I would acknowledge their concerns about having a sudden change of teacher and let them know that I want to do everything possible to make the rest of the year a happy and productive one for their children. I would ask for their suggestions and support and invite them to participate in any way they could. I would also ask each of them to tell me something special about their child so I could come to understand his or her unique qualities more quickly.

Lilly was energized by these possibilities.

The next day she went to visit the teacher whom she would be replacing and told her about my idea for the letter. "Oh you don't want to do that! Those parents come to my room every morning, and they want to talk to me. I tell them that I'm busy and that they should go to the office and make an appointment to see me . . . (pause) and you know it's strange but they never do."

The principal of the school described this teacher as a "cutting-edge" teacher—one who is doing everything right. But how was this possible when she had closed herself off to the most important avenue of communication, those who are all children's first teachers—their parents?

The teacher herself believed that she had given the parents access to herself, the classroom, and their child's education. However, because the families of her students had misunderstood her intentions, she had, in reality, created an obstacle by bringing to the situation her own set of cultural behaviors and expectations in relation to school structure and human interactions. By conveying the notion that dialogue was possible only *on her terms*, she was maintaining the existing power relations, thus preventing the kind of access she believed she was providing.

This situation is not unique. I have described it here to illustrate the kinds of obstacles that stand in the way of building true partnerships between home and school. Generally, schools are not oriented toward collaboration with families or communities. Although students and their families are taught to accommodate to the schools, only infrequently is the school open to the family's language and culture. Given the reality that teachers are facing daily in their classrooms, this is a major problem in the schools. A true partnership between home and school will not be possible until all parties, especially teachers, are committed to transcending those prescribed roles and behaviors.

My own teaching experience has shown me that most parents have a strong desire to become involved in their children's education, although they often feel ill equipped to give the needed support at home. At other times they feel ignored or criticized by the school when they try to advocate for their child.

This rejection is particularly experienced by many parents who are not members of our society's dominant culture. I am speaking here both about immigrant parents who have limited English skills or very little formal schooling in their country of origin and about other racial and cultural "minorities" or disenfranchised people in the United States, such as African Americans, Puerto Ricans, Mexican Americans, and Native Americans. Even though these minorities may have been born and raised in the United States, they are themselves products of a historically racist system of education that never offered them access to quality education.

These parents, like most parents everywhere, have high aspirations for their children as well as a desire to promote the family's culture to their children. Even though extensive research suggests the need and importance of parental involvement in education, seldom do teachers and administrators listen to the voices of the parents themselves. This remains true despite the evidence showing the primary importance of both parents' input and home and community knowledge and resources in developing a curriculum that focuses on student reality and allows for true home and school partnerships. When I use the word parents I am speaking of any important primary caregivers in the child's life. Particularly in immigrant and poor families, this often includes aunts, uncles, grandparents, or unrelated community elders.

THE NEED FOR THIS BOOK

Every classroom I enter opens my eyes anew and gives me reason to reevaluate or confirm my own approach to teaching and learning. Through classroom observations, supervision of new teachers, and hours of dialogue, I have attained a clearer understanding of the road-blocks teachers face in becoming more effective. Heavy workloads, seemingly impossible demands on their time and energy, and require-ments to comply with a preordained curriculum as mandated by their state or district sap too many teachers of their creativity and frustrate their efforts to understand their students. This problem is particularly acute for those who are teaching a culturally and linguistically diverse student population as found in many schools today.

Through my time in classrooms and in dialogue with other teach-ers, I have concluded that teachers who are struggling to meet the chal-lenge of educating all their students need to develop skills in four major areas of their work. They need to:

1. Learn to develop their classrooms as communities of learners in which each student is valued.
2. Learn how to affirm each student's cultural and linguistic iden-tity by using the knowledge each brings to school as the primary "text" for developing literacy.
3. Learn how to achieve collaborative relationships in a way that respects the student's family and community as valuable con-tributors to the educational process.
4. Learn to view themselves, in their role as teachers, as authentic human beings—not all-knowing authorities but as co-investiga-tors in a learning community.

Building Communities of Learners demonstrates that by acquiring deeper levels of understanding about the past, present, and future edu-cational realities of families, teachers can simultaneously expand their students' and their families' acquisition of literacy skills. What I am proposing here is a way to bridge the gap between what is commonly acknowledged as the important need to involve all parents in their chil-dren's education and the obstacles that leave this need largely unfilled.

The approach to education described in this book is aimed at the entire family. Specifically, it calls for building a community of learners through a collaboration among teachers, students, and their families and communities that embraces the diversity of cultures and languages that families pass on to their children. Such a collaboration promotes a posi-tive sense of personal identity and thus greatly enhances the possibilities for academic success.

HOW THIS BOOK IS ORGANIZED

Part 1 examines current trends in parental involvement in education and the hidden assumptions on which many programs that claim to have this goal are based. Next, it lays out the philosophical and theoretical rationale for building communities of learners. This rationale is grounded in a proliferating body of research and scholarship in critical pedagogy/transformative education, multicultural education, bilingual education, cooperative learning, and feminist pedagogy.

Part 2, the heart of this book, explores the role of the classroom teacher in developing a partnership with families and the community within the context of transformative education. Central to this role are participatory research, a dialogic process, and co-authorship of family books. Dialogue and the creation of books in co-authorship further enhance and validate the parent and community voice, and an integration of home and school contexts may support the emergent literacy of young students. Overall, Part 2 examines the concept of students and families as the protagonists in the story of their own lives (Ada, 1990). That is, dialogue and co-authorship of family books facilitate this role by enabling parents to participate in a reflective process with students and teachers. In this way, they critically analyze the experiences relevant to their own literacy development, their present educational relationship to the children, and their visions for achieving a home and school partnership.

Part 3 presents the intricacies and findings of a participatory research project that I conducted with first-grade parents in a multicultural, multilingual public school setting. Actual excerpts from the dialogues and examples from the books created by students and families are included.

Part 4 offers many suggestions for teachers to begin this kind of work in their own classrooms.

Part 5 presents examples of programs that engage families and communities in their own educational striving toward personal and group empowerment.

CONCLUSION

The ideas and processes described in this book represent first steps teachers can take to answer the question I posed at the beginning of this preface: *How can educators create a partnership with parents and young students that will nurture literacy and facilitate participation in the schools while celebrating and validating home culture and family and community concerns and aspirations?*

We can all help answer this important question by sharing and using what we learn from our own experience—as teachers, as students, as members of our communities, and as citizens of our increasingly diverse, ever-changing society. I hope you will read this book as if it were a conversation among colleagues and give yourself the time to reflect on the ideas and issues presented, relating them to the intellectual and personal aspects of your own work as a teacher.

ACKNOWLEDGMENTS

This book would not have been possible without the contributions, support, and love of many individuals. Building Communities of Learners has been the antithesis of a lonely experience. Indeed, my life was enriched by many along the way.

First, I would like to thank Alma Flor Ada, my mentor at the University of San Francisco who provided me with a theoretical foundation and shared with me her wealth of knowledge and strategies for working with families and for doing participatory research. She told me that this book had to be written, and I am grateful for her insistence and her beautiful Foreword. Jim Cummins generously gave his time and invaluable comments which moved me to new levels of meaning. His Afterword reminds us that the book does not end here.

Naomi Silverman, my wonderful editor at St. Martin's, refused to accept "no" when I informed her that I was not going to finish the book. Her broad understanding of educational issues, her agility with the editing pencil, and her commitment to getting a transformative book for classroom teachers into their hands quickly made this book possible.

I am grateful to Elsa Auerbach whose great book, *Making Meaning, Making Change*, was essential to my own work. The words and kindness of Henry Giroux helped me to analyze some of my own experiences and see them in light of systemic oppression.

I want to thank the co-investigators of my research study—Ena Patricia, Henry, Martha, Cynthia, and Nosisi—for allowing me to share their memories of childhood which helped us all to connect to our present educational dilemmas. Their children and many other students contributed stories and illustrations to the text. The readings, critiques, and dialogues with teachers, friends, and colleagues were critical to the completion of this book. Here I want to especially thank Laurie Olsen from California Tomorrow, Valerie Andriola Balderas, Jennifer Jue, Marguerite Conrad, Nancy Feinstein, Lillian Casteneda Vega, Linda Spatz, Catherine Walsh, Mary Poplin, Rachel Kahn-Hut, Lois Meyers, Barbara Flores, Sylvia Salgado, Graciela Spreitz, Barbara Penny-James, Mario Casteneda, and Anita DeFrantz. My good friends Dick and Dean Bunce were always totally present to hear of my successes and setbacks. My students at San Francisco State University field-tested the book and provided valuable feedback as future teachers.

I want to offer special thanks to the New College of California's visionary faculty and administration who gave me the freedom I needed during the development of a new teacher education program to finish this book as well.

During the manuscript's development, the following reviewers provided excellent suggestions and thoughtful critiques: Jim Cummins, Ontario Institute for Studies in Education; Ellen Goldsmith, NYC Technical College; Lois Meyer, Department of Elementary Education, San Francisco State University; Irma Josefine O'Neill, Teacher Education Program, SUNY–Old Westbury; Bertha Perez, San Jose State University; Catherine Walsh, University of Massachusetts at Boston; and a number of anonymous reviewers. Later in the process, the help of Diana Puglisi, my project editor at St. Martin's, was greatly appreciated.

I also thank my own children, Lucia, Pablo, and Lucca, who have always inspired my teaching and have also allowed me to teach other people's children. My parents, Miriam and Murray Singer, educators themselves, had the vision to make my childhood rich, allowing me to explore many of life's options; they always loved me and I thought I could do anything. Thanks are also due to my sister Bonnie, who visited me while I was completing the manuscript and renewed my inspiration.

Laboring alongside me through the conception, implementation, and frequent frustrations of the research and writing was Raul Nuñez. The beauty of the classroom he created and the relationships he developed with his students and their families helped make this work possible. Craig McCaleb, my husband, not only held our family together during this process, but also embraced the value of the work in every way. A carpenter by trade, he studied the readings, discussed the ideas, edited the manuscript, and at every step was indispensable to the completion of the project.

Sudia Paloma McCaleb

CONTENTS

Chapter 10   Additional Themes for Student, Family, and Community Books   159

Part 5   EXEMPLARY PROGRAMS FOR BUILDING COMMUNITIES OF LEARNERS   181

Chapter 11   Exemplary Programs for Building Communities of Learners   183

BUILDING
COMMUNITIES
of LEARNERS

part 1

BACKGROUND: A TAPESTRY OF VOICES AND IDEAS

chapter 1

An Overview of Family Involvement in Education and a Rationale for Building Communities of Learners

FAMILY INVOLVEMENT IN EDUCATION

The term *parental involvement* as generally used in American education encompasses a wide variety of approaches or activities through which parents can contribute to the school and their own child's academic progress. Educators have long recognized the important role of parents in the education of their children. The roots of parental involvement go back to a time when most mothers did not work outside the home and were generally available to meet the schedules and needs of the child and school. As early as the eighteenth century, schools distributed pamphlets offering advice to parents on childrearing practices. In the late 1880s national parent educational organizations were established, and by the 1920s and 1930s they had grown to some seventy-five in number. (For an historical review see Brim, 1959.)

Increasing rates of student failure and dropout in the last twenty years have sparked renewed interest in family education and the importance of parental involvement in the child's ability to learn. At the same time, the high influx of immigrants in many areas of the country has sparked educators to rethink some of their old assumptions about "minority" or nondominant cultures and about the ways we educate diverse populations, including how to include these families in the educational process. Although more "culturally sensitive and inclusive" curricula are beginning to be developed and implemented, this effort has been neither swift nor widespread.

Reasons for Lack of Parental Involvement

Internalized Oppression of Nondominant Groups

Traditionally in the United States, students from immigrant cultures or non-English and non-standard-English home environments have not had equal status with students from the dominant culture. The knowledge and cultural practices of their native country or their home have been devalued, since our society, like most advanced industrial societies, views knowledge as a commodity that generally can be gained only through formal schooling.

Most young children, of course, identify strongly with their families. Before attending school, the family is the child's primary reality. When students come from families whose own formal schooling has been minimal or nonexistent, these students' identification with their family reality leads them to quickly begin experiencing the contradictions between their home life and their early schooling experience. These children are immediately struck by the abundance of books in schools. In addition to the teacher's voice, these books appear to be repositories of real knowledge and the fount of real learning. When these children reflect back on their home environments, the contradictions at once become clear: "If there are many books in the school and we have so few or none in our home, that must mean that we do not know anything. Maybe my family doesn't know much, which probably means that I won't ever know much either. Maybe schooling isn't for me. Maybe I am in the wrong place. Maybe I don't belong here."

Obviously, this is a sad and discouraging scenario. When parents believe that they are "ignorant," that they have no knowledge of value to teach or share, this self-image is communicated to the children. Low self-esteem on the part of parents has a profound impact on children. Children who believe they are ignorant, having been told this all their lives, also feel less capable of learning anything new.

On the other hand, many parents deliberately communicate these thoughts to their children during their schooling years as a lesson to motivate and encourage hard work. They explain to their children that they were never given or did not take advantage of educational opportunities in their own lives. Perhaps they were poor and had to work at an early age, or perhaps there were no schools where they lived. For some, institutional racism may have prevented them from getting a good education. In any case, these parents emphasize to their children that they want and expect their lives to be better and that the children must get a good education. The parents don't want the next generation to grow up "ignorant," as they did themselves.

Socioeconomic Conditions and Relationships of Power

In 1991, Dr. John Niemeyer, president emeritus and trustee of Bank Street College of Education in New York City, together with two other educators, published *Principals Speak* (Greenspan, Niemeyer, & Seeley, 1991). This study helps us understand, on a larger level, why many parents in the United States today generally are not involved in their children's education.

The goal of the study was to present the perspective of school principals, those who generally set the tone and implement parental involvement and family-oriented programs in the school setting. The study was based on interviews with twenty-five principals who were recommended by parents and members of the communities as caring and effective leaders. One reason the researchers originally initiated the research was to explain the lack of parental involvement in the schools. After dialogue with the principals and analysis of their observations, the researchers concluded that inner-city schools, specifically those in New York City, are not structured for partnership with parents. They presented four central reasons for the lack of parental involvement in the public schools. Three of these reasons are valid but the fourth is a misreading of the family reality of most immigrant and poor children, which consists of an extended network of caregivers. This represents *not* a disintegration, but a reinterpretation of family.

1. *Transiency*. All principals recognized that building relationships of trust and working together take a lot of time and that transiency is a major obstacle to these goals. Many families move frequently, and the children are frequently forced to attend new schools.

2. *Alienation between home and school*. Social class differences are a major factor that separates teachers and administrators from families. These differences are accentuated by racial factors. Some principals emphasized that many parents are young, uneducated, or non-English speaking and are often frightened because of illegal status. Most of the principals concurred, however, that the poor parents in their schools are just as concerned about

their children as are any other parents of whatever class or stratum. They want the same things for their children as middle-class parents—a good education, good behavior, and respect for authority. Yet they often have a less clear idea of what good education is or how they can support it. The fact is that "they are in less position to get involved even if they want to" (Greenspan, Niemeyer, & Seeley, 1991, p. 11). Some principals in the study felt that parents don't trust teachers because of their own childhood experiences with schools.

3. *School-generated problems.* Some teachers are insensitive to the needs and problems of students and their families. Students sometimes bring stories home about teacher callousness that cause parents to feel distrustful of the school. One principal pointed out that many teachers are "insecure" in the inner-city schools, and, after a few bad experiences with parents based on misunderstandings, they tend to withdraw their involvement from families.

4. *Disintegration of the family.* Many children are being cared for by adults other than their natural parents. These adults may include grandparents and foster parents.

In inner-city schools, where parental involvement is often crucial to student success, these four obstacles make involvement more difficult.

All the principals in the study agreed that through their behavior and attitudes, teachers play a key role in either facilitating or obstructing good relationships with parents. Several principals also emphasized the need for adequate funding to support parental involvement programs. In analyzing the principals' dialogues, the researchers discovered that even in schools where principals truly believed in some form of parent participation, involvement was much lower than desired. They concluded that the underlying problem is an "interrelated cluster of goals, assumptions, organizational structures, concepts and mindsets underlying public education in the United States." Their view of the underlying educational paradigm is that it does not include partnership with parents. They believe that it actually "mitigates against such partnership" (Greenspan, Niemeyer, & Seeley, 1991, p. 36).

The research team concluded that the basic structure of roles and relationships in public school systems is bureaucratic rather than collaborative. This structure is based on the assumption that the task of providing education to the children has been delegated to the schools and that their role is to "deliver" this education. Ultimately, then, this leaves little room for the role of parents as the first "teachers." The study asserts that supporting and reinforcing these relationships and mindsets is the unspoken and perhaps even unconscious—but nonetheless real—functional assumption of most public school systems: schools are expected to produce "winners and losers."

This becomes a self-fulfilling prophecy for poor ethnic and linguistic minority students and their families as these assumptions are reinforced through testing, tracing, and accountability practices. Greenspan, Niemeyer, and Seeley maintain that a new model of partnership must be created in which parents are seen as a "resource instead of a nuisance." As it becomes clear that the structure of schooling in this country is of a top-down bureaucratic nature, the struggle to make the educative process a collaborative one becomes greater.

Cummins (1989) corroborates these findings. He proposes that real changes in schools will begin to take place only when the relationships of power begin to change, that is, when the voices of parents and the community are heard and the direction of the schools reflects the values of all. Throughout this book, we will see examples of how classroom teachers can invite parents to become educational resources. Accordingly, specific strategies will be discussed.

False Premises Underlying Family Education Programs

Under the direction of Elsa Auerbach in 1990, the English Family Literacy Project at the University of Massachusetts studied the most common approaches and models for family education programs and revealed what they saw as their underlying "hidden assumptions." These assumptions were examined in light of more recent research focusing on cross-cultural family literacy practices. The project suggests that programs based on stereotypes or false premises will not likely produce desirable results and may in fact have a detrimental effect on the students and their families.

Auerbach (1990) observes that many of the existing family education programs follow a "transmission of school practices model" (p. 17) in which knowledge is transmitted from teachers to children and from the schools to parents to children. The following practices were noted as the most prevalent in these transmission model programs.

1. Giving parents guidelines, materials, and training to carry out school-like activities in the home.
2. Training parents in effective parenting.
3. Teaching parents about the culture of American schooling.
4. Developing parent language and literacy through skills, grammar, and behavioral approaches.

All the programs reviewed by the English Family Literacy Project appeared to begin with the notion that there is something wrong or lacking in the family. Because educators know what parents should be doing, their job is to help parents change their ways of relating to their children and to teach them the skills needed for school-related literacy tasks. These experts begin by developing the curriculum and the practices themselves. Parents are taught to accommodate to the schools, but the schools are not expected to accommodate to the families' cultural diversity or lived reality.

After the researchers examined evidence of what actually happens in families of different class and cultural backgrounds, they concluded that this transmission of school practices is rooted in six assumptions. Based on counterevidence that emerged from their research, they view these assumptions as questionable.

Assumption 1: Home Contexts: Ethnic and linguistic minority families do not engage in literacy practices at home.

Counterevidence: Across classes and cultures, literacy is used in a wide variety of ways. It would be productive for schools to learn about the home practices of their students so they might build on the home experience. This approach is preferable to assuming inadequacies and trying to change the home practices to resemble those of school sites. Program designs could allow and include community culture to inform literacy practices. As support for this view Auerbach cites Chall and Snow (1982); Delgado-Gaitan (1987); Diaz, Moll, and Mehan (1986); Goldenberg (1984); and Taylor and Dorsey-Gaines (1988).

All the research found that even in family situations of extreme poverty, homes were rich in print material and engaged in literacy activities of many kinds on a daily basis. Parents desired to support literacy development in any way possible and frequently provided rewards for doing well in school. Immigrants were strongly aware that education was crucial to success in their new country.

Diaz, Moll, and Mehan (1986) found that the source of linguistic-minority-student problems was not language but the failure of schools and instruction to be organized in such a way as to build on the student's home and community resources and native-language abilities.

Assumption 2: Parental Roles: The success of literate children is due to parent-to-child literacy instruction and transfer of skills.

Counterevidence: Research on immigrant families indicates a complex system of family interaction wherein mutual support is given as individual family members need to adjust to cultural and language differences in their own lives. In most cases the children begin to acquire English skills through the schools and through contact with other children. Thus, they become interpreters of the outside world for adult members of the family. It may be more beneficial for schools to focus on shared literacy where teaching and learning are valued and encouraged in both directions. Assumption 2 is neither accurate nor realistic because it does not reflect the reality of the family relationship. Auerbach supports her argument with findings from the research of Delgado-Gaitan (1987); Diaz, Moll, and Mehan (1986); and Tizard, Schofield, and Hewison (1982).

Assumption 3: Family Contexts of Successful Readers: Successful readers come from home environments where parents replicate school-like tasks.

Counterevidence: There is no evidence that any single form of home literacy practice determines successful literacy development. In particular, there is no evidence that direct parental instruction to children in school-like literacy tasks accounts for school success. Studies show that a wide range of experiences and factors characterize the homes of successful readers. The most important aspect seems to be that children engage on a regular daily basis in activities integrated in socially significant ways. Auerbach points to Taylor and Dorsey-Gaines's (1988) study in which they observe that literacy events may even be occurring "at the very margins of awareness" rather than being consciously structured as specific and isolated activities. These may include family outings, a visit to the clinic, or a game of cards. It may be more productive for schools to support a variety of literacy practices and experiences that would take on significance in addressing the day-to-day concerns of the students and their families.

Assumption 4: Language Use in the Home: Children of families who do not speak the dominant language (English) at home are at a disadvantage.

Counterevidence: Research indicates that emphasizing the use of English in a home where English is not the first language may actually be detrimental to both the student and the family in general. Most important is the quality of interaction and the meaning and understanding being developed between family members. To support this view, Auerbach turns to the work of Cummins (1981) which emphasizes the importance of primary language development in the home. A strong foundation in one's native language builds a strong base for acquiring a second language. Schools would be wise to support maintenance of the student's home language because emphasizing English exclusively may undermine the development of proficiency in either the mother language or English.

Assumption 5: School versus Home Factors: The schools are doing an adequate job of teaching children, and more school-like tasks need to be done at home. It is the home that is the root cause of literacy problems.

Counterevidence: There is growing evidence that an isolated skills approach to the development of literacy (emphasizing worksheets, phonics, spelling, etc.) may actually inhibit the process. Auerbach believes that it would be a mistake for schools to insist that families attempt to duplicate in their homes what the schools are already doing. Parents should be encouraged to take a holistic approach to literacy at home and even to advocate, challenge, or change what they may see as unacceptable school programs or lack of support for students. Auerbach cites the Harvard Families and Literacy Study (Chall & Snow, 1982), which reveals that the teacher's perceptions of a student change based on the parent's willingness to advocate for the child. This study in turn showed positive consequences for the student's achievement.

Assumption 6: The Role of Social Context: Social, cultural, and economic factors are obstacles to learning and must be addressed or overcome outside the classroom.

Counterevidence: Programs that assume parental fault or inadequacies inhibit examination and discussion of the conditions that give rise to the literacy problems in the first place. Including the social context of the students and their lives at home and in the community would provide a potentially rich resource for learning and literacy development. This might include concerns about housing, health and childcare, employment, environment, and immigration. Family histories, the parent's childhood memories, and shared family activities are also important resources.

Auerbach cites the works of the following authors in presenting the counterevidence to the sixth assumption: Ada (1988); Diaz, Moll and Mehan (1986); Freire (1973); Heath (1983); Taylor (1983); Taylor and Dorsey-Gaines (1988); and Viola (1986).

As you continue to read this book, try to keep in mind Auerbach's six hidden assumptions, all of which are based on deficit views of linguistic and ethnic minority students and their families. Try to reflect on the ways in which we as teachers are lured to fall into their traps. Based on the counterevidence to these assumptions, actively work to cultivate alternative ways to embrace the realities of students and their families in your work.

Part 5 presents some examples of programs that have gone beyond these assumptions and engage families and communities in their own educational process toward personal and group empowerment.

A RATIONALE FOR BUILDING COMMUNITIES OF LEARNERS

The theoretical and philosophical underpinnings of this book are based on the work of Paolo Freire and other transformative educators in the United States who have embraced his work, including Alma Flor Ada, Elsa Auerbach, Jim Cummins, Antonia Darder, Henry Giroux, Mary Poplin, and Catherine Walsh. Although they are not part of an organized movement, through their writings and practice they all transmit a faith in the human capacity for learning, critical reflection, and action to bring about change. Many of their studies address problems of illiteracy and oppression. Each writer has motivated and changed my own work in some compelling way. They have given me the language I need to reevaluate my own teaching by reflecting from multiple perspectives on even the simplest of daily acts in which I engage with students. Their work has also inspired me to guide other teachers to approach their work with fresh optimism. They are variously known as transformative, critical, and liberatory educators.

Early in his life Paolo Freire committed himself to working with the peasant population in the impoverished northeastern part of his native Brazil. He viewed education as a way to help bring about a better world. As he began to recognize that the preliterate people with whom he was working were not receptive to formal education, he began to analyze and explore with them new approaches to literacy development. Ada (1993), a student of Freire, eloquently expresses his vision.

> He showed us that, rather than seeing ourselves as privileged owners of education, generously willing to bestow it upon others, we have to look at ourselves humbly as learners who can join in solidarity with those who are also learning, and thus bring about a shared process of liberation. By sharing the joy of learning and discovery with our students, we reaffirm the human capacity, inherent in all of us, to generate knowledge and transform the world. (p. 25)

In addition to the work being carried out based on Freire's teachings, a rich variety of educational philosophies, approaches, and strategies for program implementation have gained much recognition and many supporters among classroom teachers. All have been essential in my own work. These include multicultural education, bilingual education, whole language, cooperative learning, and feminist pedagogy. Although these approaches may be implemented and integrated in conjunction with a Freirian participatory approach to education, this is not often the case. All of these philosophies influence direct classroom pedagogies. I will define them later in this chapter and will follow those definitions with a discussion of their potential application to a Freirian-based philosophy.

Paolo Freire, Critical Pedagogy, and Transformative Education

Freire's experiences with the development of adult literacy in Brazil provide valuable knowledge and models to educators working in the United States during the present period of social and educational change.

Early in his work, Freire (1973) rejected mechanistic forms of teaching literacy, which for teachers in the United States might include phonics and standard basal reader approaches. He felt that it was important to teach the students to read within the context of their awakening consciousness.

> We wanted a literacy program which would be an introduction to the democratization of culture, a program with men and women as its Subjects rather than patient recipients, a program which itself would be an act of creation, capable of releasing other creative acts, one in which students would develop the impatience and vivacity which characterize search and invention. (p. 43)

Freire was convinced that, if students were treated as the subjects of their own learning, they would achieve the ability to express, through language, the knowledge that represented their own relation to reality. His methods were based on dialogue. He believed that "When the two 'poles' of the dialogue are thus linked by love, hope, and mutual trust, they can join in critical search for something. Only dialogue truly communicates" (p. 45).

Freire believes that in the absence of a sincere dialogue between the teacher and student, the relationship can become one of domestication and will be devoid of respect and love. This dialogue must be about situations that are concrete to the lives of the participants.

"Banking Education"

Both Freire and Giroux assert that true knowing and knowledge are not possible within the structure of traditional education because dialogue and reflection are not an integral part of traditional curricula. Freire (1970) believes that knowledge is imposed on students, and, like empty vessels waiting to be filled, they are generally passive in the way they receive that knowledge. He also sees traditional education as a way to domesticate and thus dominate students. Giroux (1983) concurs and sees within traditional education a "hidden curriculum" through which students are taught to follow rules and not ask questions. Giroux (1990b) observes that discussion of issues that might challenge teacher-based assumptions is absent from the classroom. Freire (1973) calls these characteristics of traditional education "banking education"—the process through which students receive deposits on a variety of typically disconnected subjects and are expected to mouth back the information at a later time.

Ideology, Knowledge, and Power

This traditional pedagogy not only silences creativity but also prevents the integration of knowledge with the students' own experiences and the reality of their world. For Giroux (1983), traditional educational theory does not address the critical issues of ideology, knowledge, and power. Administrators and teachers spend many hours developing curriculum models based on principles of control and measurement. Their focus becomes the teaching of basic isolated skills. Thus, schools are seen as social sites with a dual curriculum. The first is clearly stated, and the second is the hidden curriculum in which schools segregate students by race, social class, or gender and place value on the knowledge of a single culture (Western European) and a single class (upper/middle).

Poplin (1991) concurs when she describes the current structure of schooling as primarily benefiting privileged and middle-class youngsters. "Schools attempt to reproduce those classes so that the children of poverty are educated in such a way that they remain in poverty" (p. 8).

For Freire (1973), education must ultimately be a process of liberation and humanization. It cannot be an instrument that teachers use to manipulate the students. The students must be invited to "recognize and unveil reality critically" (p. 102). Both the students and the teachers are engaged in dialogue about their worlds.

Dialogue and Problem Posing

The central pedagogies of transformative or critical education are *dialogue* and *problem posing*. The problems must be real-life concerns that the students engage in for critical reflection. Through this process, students come to see and understand how they exist in the world. The teacher is present not only as an observer or a guide but also as a co-participant in the ongoing dialogue. "Critical pedagogy," states Giroux (1983) "must provide the conditions that give students the opportunity to speak with their own voices, to authenticate their own experiences" (p. 203).

Poplin (1991) builds on this theory by emphasizing that critical pedagogy is concerned primarily with ways to educate citizens to "live responsibly in a free and democratic state." These educators recognize the political nature of schools, and their purpose is to make the world more just by teaching students to think and act critically.

In a transformative classroom, students are encouraged to develop their own voices in interaction with the voices of others and to participate in the democracy of the classroom. Poplin states that the teacher's role is "to encourage this democratic process, to provide opportunities for the development of voice and to bring forth voices that can lead to action in the larger society" (p. 8).

In a transformative classroom, the teacher aims to bring out the voices of all the students. Transformative education struggles against the feelings of impotence and lethargy experienced by those who have not yet spoken or been heard and works to use "the diversity inherent in the U.S. to create a more just and more whole society" (Poplin, 1991, p. 9).

The students must begin to see the world as an active reality that is continuously transforming. They become motivated to change from passive, subservient listeners to active, critical co-investigators (Freire, 1970). For Freire, education is not directed toward freedom; rather, it is the living practice of freedom.

Transformative educators attempt to facilitate a critical capacity within the classroom while promoting the integration of students, families, communities, and the world. Classroom teachers have the opportunity to create classroom environments that offer opportunities for analyzing and debating problems on a daily basis. The classroom can be the microcosm where democracy is learned, practiced, and constantly reinvented.

> Democracy and democratic education are founded on faith in people, on the belief that they not only can but should discuss the problems of their country, of their continent, of their world, their work, the problems of democracy itself. Education is an act of love, and thus an act of courage. It cannot fear the analysis of reality or, under pain of revealing itself as a farce, avoid creative discussion. (Freire, 1973, p. 38)

Giroux (1989) emphasizes that the present reality of American schooling is highly oppressive. He believes that our educational system offers little for those who are not "rich," white, or native speakers of English. "Marginalized students must locate themselves in their own histories as part of the task of learning the knowledge and skills they will need to shape the world in which they live" (p. 228). "Marginalized" students are those who do not fit into the dominant culture and whose voices are continually not heard. He speaks about the need to reclaim the schools in the interest of "extending democratic possibilities, combating domestic tyranny, and preventing assaults on human freedom and dignity" (p. 229). For transformative educators, a discussion of schools is very much intertwined with a discussion of society in general and democracy specifically. Giroux reminds us of John Dewey's belief that democracy is a way of life that has to be made and remade by each generation.

Teachers as Transformative Intellectuals

Within Giroux's vision, teachers must be seen as transformative intellectuals who must be given time not only to plan and reflect with others about the theory that informs their practice but also to learn about the community in which their schools are located. They need to be able to create classrooms in which students can understand and appreciate cultural and linguistic differences. Teachers also need the power to shape the curriculum that is suited to the interests of the students they actually teach. Schools must begin to close the gap between "what they teach and the real world." The identity of the students, their knowledge, cultures, and communities, need to form the basic structure of the curriculum.

Central to Giroux's critical theory of education reform is the assumption that knowledge and power are inseparable. He believes that school curriculum policies should draw on the resources of a culturally diverse student population. Teaching practices that include only one group's knowledge might serve to silence rather than empower the students who are located in cultural worlds that exist at the margins of the dominant culture. While these silenced students can still learn, he cautions that unfortunately they also learn that they don't count.

When as teachers we can begin to critically engage the distinctive experiences that students bring to school, we can help them to understand and move beyond their experiences. This is the essence of transformative or critical education. Teachers must educate students to believe they can make a difference in the world. As already stated, for Freire this kind of pedagogy is integral to his vision of human freedom or emancipation.

In the following chapters, we put the philosophies of Freire, Giroux, and Poplin into practice for classroom teachers as the voices of Ada, Auerbach, and Cummins also become interwoven.

Emerging Philosophies and Classroom Practices

The emerging philosophies discussed in this section have the potential to chart a new course in education. Strategies that stem from these philosophies have already been embraced by many classroom teachers, and in some cases by entire school districts as well. Although these pedagogies are not necessarily transformative in and of themselves, they do provide a theoretical framework within which teachers can build a transformative classroom that will speak to the salient issues of their students.

Multicultural Education

For the classroom teacher, the most popular conceptualization of the term *multicultural education* is the periodic incorporation of cultural artifacts displayed on bulletin boards and the celebration of cultural and national holidays complete with food and song. In this way, students are given a "taste" of the many cultural groups that make up our community, state, and world. The time devoted to each cultural group often coincides with an official celebration such as Black History Month, Cinco de Mayo, or the Chinese New Year. Each group is viewed as a separate entity rather than as a collection of human beings whose contributions to the history of the country and the world are interrelated to the contributions and experiences of the other cultural groups.

Some educators believe that the concept of multicultural education is appropriate only for students in urban public schools. This attitude is paternalistic in the sense that only once a year does it welcome the culture of the students in a positive light. In truth, multicultural education is education for everyone. In this rapidly shrinking world, human beings must be able to understand and respect each other's differences. This consciousness must be infused throughout the curriculum. Students will not be truly educated if they don't receive an education that enables them to discover their own place in history.

Sonia Nieto, in her book *Affirming Diversity* (1992), has proposed a broad and more authentic multicultural education, one that is rooted in critical pedagogy.

> Multicultural education is a process of comprehensive school reform and basic education for all students. It challenges and rejects racism and other forms of discrimination in schools and society and accepts and affirms the pluralism (ethnic, racial, linguistic, religious, economic, and gender, among others) that students, their communities, and teachers represent. Multicultural education permeates the curriculum and instructional strategies used in schools, as well as the interactions among teachers, students and parents, and the very way that schools conceptualize the nature of teaching and learning. Because it uses critical pedagogy as its underlying philosophy and focuses on knowledge, reflection and action (praxis) as the basis for social change, multicultural education furthers the democratic principles of social justice. (p. 208)

This definition encourages the opportunity for all voices to be heard in a classroom. The students' cultural and linguistic backgrounds, as well as their families and community, are incorporated into the classroom text for exploration and understanding on a daily basis, and not just during specific holiday times. Multicultural education permeates the curriculum and represents democracy in practice.

Inconsistencies are present even in schools that think they are approaching education from a multicultural perspective. Some schools have multicultural teachers who visit classes once a week for half an hour, thereby relieving the classroom teacher of this responsibility. Other schools consider themselves antiracist because they have a multicultural curriculum in place. Rarely, however, are these schools indeed free of racism. For example, in most schools students of color predominate in low-track learning groups or classes; few will appear in higher track classes. Our schools reflect the society outside, and all students inside live in this society. Antiracism has to be taught. The racism students learn from living in the larger society needs to be unlearned; schools cannot just pretend that it does not exist and hope that it will go away.

The study of history needs to include everyone's history, even the painful parts of that history. In many cases, the curriculum is sanitized; that is, only certain historical figures are considered appropriate for school teaching. Dr. Martin Luther King, for example, is a hero who has been shaped to fit school needs. His militancy, his vocal opposition to the Vietnam War, and his attacks on capitalism are never discussed; the almost exclusive focus is on his "Dream."

True multicultural education is critical pedagogy. Students do not simply receive knowledge from the teacher; rather, they are introduced to multiple perspectives and are encouraged to compare, critique, evaluate, and use their own experiences to create a new reality in which they have the power to take action that will change situations of injustice and positively impact their own lives. True multicultural education implies a restructuring of schools in many of their most basic forms.

Bilingual Education

By bilingual education we generally mean the use of two languages for instruction. For example, in the most common model of a Spanish bilingual program, a transitional bilingual program, young children are instructed in their native language, Spanish, only until they understand enough English to be transitioned into English-speaking classrooms or "exited" out of Spanish-language instruction. At the same time, part of their instruction is in English, so that they are simultaneously acquiring English skills.

A *submersion* bilingual education program, which is often referred to as sink or swim, is one in which students who have a home language other than English and are often new arrivals to the United States are literally thrown into an all-English environment with no native language support. Whereas in some schools this approach is used because no instructional language resources are available, in other schools it is intentionally designed to eradicate the student's home language.

Immersion bilingual education is an approach whereby students enter clusively for a few years until they gain adequate skills in the second language. The primary language becomes integrated once again until the two languages of instruction gradually balance out the instructional day. This method has been successfully used in Canada to teach English-speaking students French. The method strives toward complete bilingualism.

Two-way bilingual education is a model in which English-dominant students are integrated with, for instance, Spanish-speaking students. The language of instruction is Spanish. The expectation is that both groups become bilingual. Instruction is primarily in Spanish, which is the lower status language in this society. The Spanish-dominant students are given the opportunity to develop their primary language skills to the highest level (instead of losing their native language), while the English-speaking students acquire second-language skills by modeling after their classmates. Research demonstrates that Spanish-speaking students who have a strong foundation in their first language will attain higher levels of academic success. This is the place where they begin to develop their higher level skills and critical thinking skills—skills that transfer easily to the second language.

The goal of a *bilingual maintenance* program is to maintain the students' first language while they acquire English fluency. This skill is achieved by continuing to teach subjects in the child's first language and continually increasing the first-language level of development. It does not imply the maintenance of Spanish to the exclusion of English; rather, it recognizes the value of students' becoming truly bilingual.

How do individual district schools or classroom teachers decide which method of bilingual education should be implemented? The answer lies within the realm of philosophy and ultimately within a vision of what society might look like. If our vision is one of a truly pluralistic society in which differences are considered to be riches and language is viewed as an expression of culture and self-identity, then, of course, multiple languages will be valued. Within a transformative pedagogy, all students are encouraged to develop their own language because it is an expression of who they are and places them in their own history. New languages, like new knowledge, can only be built on the firm foundation of what is already known and familiar. Maintaining one's own language also continues the links with one's culture and family. Students who have been forced by schooling to abandon their home language have frequently suffered tragic repercussions because of the breakdown in the family and community possibilities for communication.

This issue is extremely complicated, and in order to tackle it we need a clear understanding of the community in which the program is implemented. Based on my own experience and data gathered through research, I have come to the conclusion that bilingual maintenance and two-way immersion programs hold the greatest potential for transformative educators. Both respect the knowledge and skills that a student brings to school. Instead of attempting to cut students off from who they are, they invite them to cross the borders of learning both intellectually and emotionally, and to affirm multiple perspectives by cultivating multiple identities.

Whole Language

Whole language learning is a meaning-based holistic approach to reading and writing based primarily on student experiences and on what students already know. Reading is not simply the identification and pronunciation of words; it is also a process in which students construct their own meanings. The readers actually construct their own text to parallel the text being read and, in the creation of this text, incorporate their own experiential knowledge, beliefs, and values. Students are encouraged to ask questions and to seek their own answers while also being entrusted to choose what they want to read. This makes learning personal and social.

The practice of whole language in English-speaking countries like New Zealand, Britain, Canada, and Australia predates the movement in the United States. The term *whole language learning* became popularized in Canada so that Canadians could differentiate the kinds of teaching they were developing from the isolated skills approach (such as basal readers) that they saw popularized in the United States. Whole language in New Zealand, Britain, Canada, and Australia has undergone an evolution in thought and practice. For many teachers in the United States, joining this movement has meant risking their jobs. What makes whole language so revolutionary and such a threat?

When teachers begin to reflect on what they are doing and when they make changes in the ways they teach, they often discover that school policies and mandates are no longer acceptable and that they are even morally wrong. The contradictions become glaring. Whole language is a growing movement throughout the United States and the world, and is having a profound effect in classrooms as teachers themselves begin to take action toward change. Strong advocates of whole language argue that it is not just a method but a set of beliefs (Edelsky, Altwerger, & Flores, 1991).

Whole language teachers do not push or rush students to begin to learn to read. They see "readiness" for reading when the classroom language experiences are real and students are excited and motivated. They support their students by building on the knowledge they bring into the classroom. Whole language learning does not require a hierarchy of skill sequences that must be learned, nor does it teach spelling as a separate subject. The students begin by inventing their own spelling, and they come to learn the rules organically by taking risks and developing their self-confidence. They begin to move toward conventional spelling as they continue to write and focus their writing on real ideas and the purpose and audience for which they are writing.

Ken and Yetta Goodman, major spokespersons for whole language in the United States, are widely read by American teachers and have invited many teachers to take the plunge in their own work.

> Whole language is producing a holistic reading and writing curriculum which uses real, authentic literature and real books. It puts learners in control of what they read and write about. But it also produces new roles for teachers and learners and a new view of how teaching and learning are related. Whole language reemphasizes the need for curriculum integrated around problem solving in science and social studies with pupils generating their own questions and answering them collaboratively. Whole language revalues the classroom as a democratic learning community where teachers and pupils learn together and learn to live peacefully together. That's made it possible and necessary for whole language to integrate within it many compatible educational concepts. (Goodman, 1992)

Indeed, whole language can be extremely compatible with a transformative approach to education.

For many teachers, becoming a critical whole language educator will imply giving up some of their formerly held beliefs and assumptions about learning, including the notion that language is a system of parts to be learned by sequentially perfecting each separate skill. As students become engaged in real language use in which they are the subject of their learning, they develop their skills and become better at using language. Mistakes become resources for learning.

The theory that underlies the practice of whole language educators permits the classroom to be a liberating experience, to be potentially transformative. However, what emerges from the classroom frequently does not reflect that inherent potential.

> And what makes whole language truly revolutionary is not just the built-in potential for curriculum rich in critique. It is the built-in potential coupled with what whole language is an alternative to. Whole language eliminates the grouping for reading and the tracking that ensures unequal access to "cultural capital" (i.e. certain texts, vocabulary, knowledge, analyses). It devalues the major language based devices for stratifying people. It makes teachers the authors (not "deliverers" or "managers") of curriculum. In other words, it helps subvert the school's role in maintaining a stratified society. (Edelsky, Altwerger, & Flores, 1991, p. 54)

Whole language theory is continually evolving as new research emerges and elucidates learning issues. The teacher's role in this process is essential. In addition to classroom teachers, parents, grandparents, and siblings are also teachers, according to whole language theory. It is important that teachers understand that business and political interests are continually trying to undermine the whole language movement. For example, a myriad of systems and products such as Whole Language Basal Kits have been developed in an attempt to exploit a market and co-opt the movement. Classroom teachers should realize that whole language cannot be packaged and that they are the only ones who can bring it to life, helping it nurture fairness and democracy. At the same time educators should also take an honest look at both whole language and other process-oriented philosophies within their school and community context in order to determine whether they are in fact addressing the needs of diverse language and cultural groups within the classroom.

A challenge to the whole language philosophy and strategies has come from a number of educators who are particularly concerned about the needs of students from the nondominant culture. Lisa Delpit (1988) and Maria De la Luz Reyes (1992) emphasize the need for clear expectations for diverse students who are being taught to acquire specific skills. In particular, they object to the sometimes vague and amorphous drift that tends to affect a whole language program. Teachers must share their expertise with students, and not just take a back seat. Teachers cannot simply assume that through an ongoing whole language-oriented process students will gain all the needed skills without being directly guided and coached.

> Many liberal educators hold that the primary goal for education is for children to become autonomous, to develop fully who they are in the classroom setting without having arbitrary, outside standards forced upon them. This is a very reasonable goal for people whose children are already participants in the culture of power and who have already internalized its codes. (Delpit, 1988, pp. 488–489)

Although whole language may well provide universal access to education and allow the voices and needs of all groups to be heard, educators and parents from diverse ethnic and linguistic groups have often been silenced in this debate.

> A carte blanche acceptance of any program reduces the likelihood that needed modifications for diverse learners will be made. . . . Failure to address the needs of non-mainstream students is not due to a conscious mission but to an established tradition of ignoring differences among learners. . . . This promotes an ethnocentric definition of literacy based on strategies designed for mainstream students as the model for all learners. (Reyes, 1992, pp. 427–428)

Cooperative Learning

Cooperative learning refers to the structuring of classrooms so that students work together in small cooperative groups. Classroom teachers may choose from a wide spectrum of strategies ranging from very formal and clearly articulated classroom structures, which generally address one area of content learning such as science, to open-ended and informal structures (such as writing a story or producing a skit), which apply cooperative learning across subject areas and grade levels. Kagan (1986) describes four major formal cooperative learning methods: peer practice, jigsaw, cooperative projects, and curriculum-specific approaches.

Some researchers contend that marginalized students attain higher achievement levels when they learn in the context of a cooperative classroom (Kagan, 1986). When these students are forced into a competitive situation, they often lose their spirit of motivation. In competitive and individualistic types of classrooms, males from the dominant culture are more likely to succeed, while females and students from lower status groups are likely to do more poorly. Unfortunately, most schools throughout the country continue to rely on transmission models of education. As a nation, we profess democratic ideals. Indeed, an inevitable tension exists between freedom and authority, both of which are necessary in the classroom. However, too many of our schoolrooms are characterized as competitive and autocratic, an approach that appears to be especially detrimental to the academic success of students who are not members of the dominant culture. According to Kagan (1986),

> What appears to be long term minority student deficiency in basic language skills can be overcome by transforming the social organization of the classroom. Thus, the gap in achievement between majority and minority students is best not attributed to personal deficiencies of minority students, but rather to the relatively exclusive reliance in public schools on competitive and individualistic classroom structures. (pp. 246–247)

In many instances, teachers believe that their students are engaged in cooperative learning just because they are sitting at the same table. They may even be filling in the blank spaces on a ditto summary sheet.

> Cooperative learning in transformative classrooms doesn't "look like" a methodology being practiced. The cooperation in these classrooms "looks" more like a family, complete with disputes and voluntary changing of groups. To act as a family, to come to know one another and ourselves as we are known is critical to the education enterprise. (Poplin, 1992, p. 28)

The Feminist Perspective

Because much of this book emphasizes the need to build our classroom environment and teaching around the student's subjective knowledge and personal experience, we must recognize the contributions of feminist thinking to this kind of perspective. For example, feminist thinking has emphasized the importance of human feelings, lived experience, intuition, and people's ability to construct their own knowledge. It has accentuated the importance of relationships themselves in order to facilitate the process of learning and transformation. Moreover, it has acknowledged the relative nature of what people believe to be truth, and the need to understand the relationship between power and social constructs about "truth." Feminism has confronted us with how so many people's truths have been silenced in the course of their daily lives, in the academic world, and in the institutions of our society. This, of course, includes our schools and classrooms.

Feminist thought has underscored the value of what have traditionally been seen as women's strengths—sympathy, empathy, skills in building and maintaining relationships, passion, and "women's ways of knowing," such as intuition and the spirit (Belensky et al., 1986). In addition, feminists have compellingly reframed some of what has been traditionally seen as women's "weakness"—their "sensitivity" and their "emotionality" (Miller, 1976). In short, feminist thinking has been an integral part of the interdisciplinary movement to question the paradigms of traditional pedagogy. It is part of the growing push to evaluate professional and intellectual integrity and to gain a consciousness of how power and culture affect knowledge. Feminist pedagogy requires teachers to know and question themselves honestly and to understand, respect, and integrate the experiences and knowledge of their students and their community into the classroom reality. Personal experience is the necessary starting point for understanding.

A feminist perspective recognizes the limitations inherent in "objective" truth. These include the separation of the creation of knowledge from emotion and experience. A feminist perspective also recognizes different characteristics of the universal and the individual. Universal knowledge is constructed by the dominant and most powerful group in society and is imposed on students by the system of schooling. The individual knowledge created by nondominant groups, including the majority of students in our public schools, is rarely recognized, appreciated, or validated.

On our best days, we as classroom teachers are continually interacting and empathizing with our students, and reflecting on their steady stream of activity and emotions. One of the most challenging aspects of classroom teaching is to maintain a dynamic balance between thought, feeling, and action. To help achieve this balance, teachers must handle a multiplicity of relationships; these relationships involve thirty students and their families, as well as co-workers and administrators.

Working with students means that teachers must recognize the context of a student's learning. In turn, teachers must also work with their families rather than according to some external objective assumption of who the students are, what they should know, and how teachers might "connect" with them.

In the main, classroom teachers do not speak the language of educational theorists; often their thoughts remain private and so are unknown to the public. Knowledge shared among colleagues is often intuitive. This kind of knowledge is not rewarded or recognized in professional literature, which obliges teachers to identify the steps of their thinking and rewards "universalistic" rather than "individual or relational" knowledge (Gilligan, 1982). Little is written about teachers' experiences in the classroom and what they are learning from their students and about themselves.

Unlike women in other professions, women in teaching generally do not feel they have to be like men. The classroom needs to reflect an integration of the masculine and feminine approaches to knowledge. While the masculine approach tends to be linear and fact-oriented, Mary Poplin (1991) states, "The values attributed to the feminine and evident in the transformative classroom include passion; subjectivity; intuition; aesthetics; care; spirituality; community; and authenticity" (p. 9).

Intuitive knowledge has always been distinctly absent in the public language of schooling (Belensky et al., 1986). It is now crucial to balance the appreciation of "fact" with acknowledgment of the context that shapes our "facts." Similarly, we must learn to balance validation of analytical thinking with support for the intuitive knowledge and energies that a feminist perspective is most capable of contributing to the transformation of a classroom.

Are the values expressed by Poplin discussed either in faculty meetings or in teacher education programs? How would the teaching profession in general be different if these values were acknowledged and nurtured? A feminist pedagogy constantly strives to realize new possibilities for teaching and learning, giving special thought and planning to each individual student. In contrast, in the traditional perspective on schools, student needs and realities are viewed in relation to an objective standard. This striving for objectivity dehumanizes students and their families and causes many to withdraw from the educational process, either emotionally or physically.

> Transformative teachers describe the enormous personal pain of "giving grades" as the clash between two voices, on the one hand what one logically deserves relative to others (justice) versus what grade one should get for trying, what one needs for their development (care). (Poplin, 1992, p. 23)

Teaching from the feminist perspective opposes the prevalent compartmentalization and specialization that force teachers to view subjects in isolation. Through the traditional perspective, classroom teaching has become separated from questions that examine the meaning of life and justice and that revolve around caring for each other and the environment. Among these questions are the following. Where is the spirit? What is spirituality? What source of energy enables us to help transform the world, our communities, and, as the first step, our classrooms, and how do we sustain that energy?

In traditional classrooms, teachers are told that they are responsible for imparting knowledge to students who are there primarily to receive and accept that knowledge. Preestablished curricula often prevent teachers from taking the time to understand their students and to develop authentic relationships with them. Such relationships, of course, imply a give and take. Thus, if students are asked to share of themselves, it is equally important for teachers to communicate who *they* are to their students. Within this relationship, teacher and student affect each other, making both parties capable of change. However, teachers are often led to believe that, in order to participate in this kind of relationship, they must relinquish their authority and therefore will "lose control." But Poplin (1992) warns that the teachers who generally have the greatest problems with "behavior management" (euphemistically named) are "those who do not know their students in an authentic way. To some degree they are unauthentic, even with themselves" (p. 30).

Within a feminist perspective, in addition to intuitive knowledge, all students and teachers are also capable of aesthetic creation. Are we giving our students adequate avenues for expression, or do we minimize their opportunity to enter into the arts? For many students, aesthetic expression can be the key they need to enter other areas of learning. Transformative educators must bring the aesthetic into the classroom and offer their students multiple opportunities in drawing, painting, singing, listening to music, dancing, and drama.

Teachers who teach from a feminist perspective may encounter difficulties in a system that is predominantly male-oriented. As noted earlier, classrooms should reflect an integration between the masculine and feminine, combining the cognitive and analytically oriented approach with the intuitive and the aesthetic. Nurturing the feminine side of our teaching will allow us greater possibilities for discovering the wholeness of each of our students and for helping both teachers and students to be all they can be.

FAMILY LITERACY PROGRAMS

Throughout this book, the term *family education* or *family literacy* refers to the collaboration between the family, community, and school in support of the student's emerging literacy skills. For many families, this effort may involve children and adults learning to read and write together or seeking to improve their reading and writing skills. This is a true form of parental involvement because, during their own process of collaboration and learning, the adults are modeling authentic and positive learning behaviors while at the same time supporting their children's growing academic skills.

The focus in this work is on family education and parental involvement during the period of early literacy development. Although the success of all children and all families is clearly desirable, I have chosen to emphasize the multicultural and multilingual school environments for which a clear pedagogical vision and practice are becoming more urgent. What interplay do we find between the school and classroom pedagogy and the home and surrounding community? Four basic principles must lay the foundation for this new work.

1. *Teachers and their students together are co-participants in the learning process.* The teacher can no longer be considered the repository of all valid knowledge. Students have ways of knowing and "ways with words" (Heath, 1983). Learning may be defined as an interchange of ideas and experiences that are to be shared and to be the source of some reflection. This sharing helps us validate the language, cultural differences, learning styles, and behavioral expectations and values of the family and community.

2. *New knowledge is built on old knowledge.* Knowledge is dynamic, which means that it is continually undergoing evolution. True learning takes place when students are involved in both the creation and utilization of knowledge. When learning starts with the student's own life, we have a grounding for new experiences from which new meanings can be constructed.

3. *Parents and communities need to be seen as equal contributors of understanding and knowledge to the educative process.* Power relationships that presently exist in the school structure must be opened up so that parents can become participants in their children's learning by contributing their oral or written words, ideas, and experiences as part of the text of schooling.

4. *Through analysis and critique, all people are capable of engaging in actions that may transform their present realities.* Antonio Machado in his beautiful poem uttered the words, "Caminante, no hay camino, se hace camino al andar." [Traveler, there is no road, we make the road by walking.] These words, we make the road by walking, later became the title of a book by Paolo Freire and Miles Horton (1991). The words affirm the belief that there is no set way or formula to be followed, but if we as teachers fully commit ourselves to the process and respond authentically to what we see and feel, we can re-create the present and thus transform the future.

How can educators begin to discover the knowledge that exists within a family and community? How can a teacher begin to understand what a student knows and thinks about? How can a critical understanding of that knowledge empower students to take action that will change and improve their own lives and those of the people in their communities?

How can schools, and particularly classroom teachers, begin to integrate the multiple forms of family and community knowledge into classroom study? I offer this book as a contribution to achieving these goals.

BEGINNING THE PROCESS OF CHANGE

In recent years, as a supervisor of new teachers and teacher candidates, I have had the opportunity to visit dozens of urban classrooms. I have seen many teachers engaging in exciting classroom activities such as well-developed thematic units, interactive journal writing, literature-based reading, and extensive art projects. Through in-depth dialogues with teachers, I have discovered that many teachers are focused on, and rightfully concerned about, what they view as their students' deficits. In what ways are students lacking? How are they behind, and why do they believe it is impossible to count on any support from the home? In a conversation with a fifth-grade teacher about the possible merits of cooperative learning, which was absent in his classroom, he confided to me that he didn't believe in cooperative learning strategies because "children don't know anything." He told me that he was responsible for the curriculum and for teaching the children what they had to know. "If I put them in groups, they'll have nothing to teach each other." He added, "Maybe at the end of the year when they know something I'll try that."

This conversation prompted me to investigate what students actually do know and how they theorize about "knowledge" and "knowing." What place does this concept have in their own lives and those of their families and communities? I was anxious to explore how educators might shift the traditional technocratic orientation of education toward a more participatory, critical, and creative approach. How can educators begin to change the focus of education from the "transmission" of knowledge to the concept of building communities of learners through a collaboration among teachers, students, families, and community?

part 2

INITIATING HOME AND SCHOOL PARTNERSHIPS

chapter 2

Teachers as Facilitators of Home–School Relationships

Classroom teachers have the ability as well as the responsibility to facilitate and help strengthen the relationships of students with their families and communities. The strength of this relationship affects a student's positive self-identity. The student's cultural life becomes an important aspect of classroom learning and, as a result, the possibility for academic success is enhanced.

Although many schools are apparently committed to programs that invite community input and strive to reflect family values, many ethnic and linguistic minority parents are intimidated by the large, institutional structure of the school and schooling. For some, this feeling may be based on unhappy memories of their own schooling experiences. Others may be negative because when they tried to approach the school they were coldly received, spoken to in a language they did not understand, or confusedly turned away. Many of these parents would prefer to relate to their child's own teacher. A recent research project carried out by the Institute for Education in Transformation (1992) studied problems in schooling from the "inside." The year-long study, the product of collaboration with all members of the school community, revealed the following:

> Parents say they want an honest dialogue between themselves and their children's teachers. Even more important, many parents fear that poor relationships between teachers and their children damage their children's sense of confidence and vitality. Students of color, especially older students often report that their teachers, school staff and other students neither like nor understand them. When relationships in schools are poor . . . a sense of depression and hopelessness exists. (1992, p. 12)

The classroom teacher sees the students every day and so plans appropriate teaching and follows their daily progress. Children are part of that teacher's life, thoughts, and often preoccupations. Many teachers take their students' work home at night to read and write responses as well as to create new materials and to plan curricula. If we accept the notion that the parent is the child's first teacher, then it follows that the teacher is the second.

IDENTITIES AND CONTRADICTIONS

A child's educational possibilities are impeded when these two teachers are seen to be in contradiction, that is, when the child feels that one of her teachers does not value the other. A child is often forced to make difficult choices about whose teachings she is going to accept and whose she will reject. When the values and teachings of the home and the school are quite different, serious intergenerational conflicts can result. In the best of circumstances, the student need not be pulled in two opposing directions and feel that allegiance or respect for one teacher negates the value of the other.

As students grow older and begin to mature, the peer culture and peer relationships take on major importance. Feeling a strong need to belong, they do not want to be isolated or ridiculed in any way. Some young people begin to feel ashamed of the culture and language of their own parents or grandparents. Many recent immigrant students want to be Americans and to feel that they are "real" Americans; thus, many of these students see a need to separate from their home culture. They want to be able to define their own identities as better reflecting their new culture. While some students accept their bicultural identities, others want to deny their home culture completely. Some believe that, if they take on one identity, then they will not be able to function properly in the other. One Latina elementary teacher explains it this way.

> Students of color must learn to negotiate their own culture to try to "fit into" the dominant culture. This can be a difficult and painful process because students of color feel they must reject their own culture in order to assimilate. Conversely, if they choose to maintain their own culture, they may be perceived as defiant or nonconformist. The struggle that these stu-

dents experience stems from the subtle racism that has been institutional-
ized in American schools. American schools have socialized all students to
fit into one dominant culture with no regard to their own home culture.
Even though many teachers reach out to their students of color and expand
the curriculum in new directions, students of color still feel they must
choose between their culture or the dominant culture. This is the essence of
being bicultural. (Institute for Education in Transformation, 1992, p. 28)

We are beginning to witness the tragedy that may result when students reject the home culture. As students pull themselves away from
their roots and family ties, they need to find or become part of another
group for support and care. Growing numbers of young people are
succumbing to the attractions of gang involvement. This is one of the
more serious behavioral consequences for students who have cut off
communication and reject the values with which they were raised and
nurtured.

VALIDATING MULTIPLE IDENTITIES: FIRST STEPS

Classroom teachers have not only the honor but also the obligation to
examine and decide how they can begin to facilitate a partnership with
the student's family and community so that the student can become an
integrated, self-assured human being. This responsibility cannot be
handed over to historical probability, the society at large, or a conservative school administration.

A teacher can begin to reach out to families in many ways, which
will in turn help the students build their own self-esteem, an indispensable ingredient for most learning. A primary factor to be considered in
how a teacher might begin to do so is the student's age and grade level.
Although many strategies are appropriate for younger students who are
just entering the formal world of literacy, a teacher can use the same
strategies appropriate for older students.

This relationship can begin during the first weeks of school. If the
parents themselves bring their children to school, the teachers can make
immediate personal contact. Teachers can express their pleasure in
meeting the parents and invite them into the classroom to see how the
students are learning. Some parents will even respond to a sincere
request for classroom participation.

Letters Sent Home

In most schools, letters sent home are the initial form of communication from the teacher. Teachers should help ensure that the letters
are written in the home language of the child. This will immediately

demonstrate the teacher's respect for the family's language and an attitude of caring. In some schools it is important for teachers to establish relationships with other school personnel, a parent, or an appropriate community person with whom they can develop an ongoing translation exchange. If teachers think about their communications in advance, it will be somewhat easier for them to arrange for a translation. Here is an example of a letter that one first-grade teacher signed and sent home.

Dear Parents of Room 4,

It has been a pleasure to begin to get to know your children during this first week of school. They are so bright-eyed and seem so ready to learn. I know we are going to have an exciting year together.

As your child's first teacher, I know that you have taught her a great deal. I hope that we can talk soon and that you can share with me some of the ways in which you have taught your child at home. I'm sure that you will have good suggestions about what you want your child to learn at school and how I, as her new teacher, can help her to learn better.

We have a bulletin board in our classroom which we have saved for pictures of our students and their families. We would love for each student to bring to the classroom a picture of the special adults in her life. In that way the students will feel your presence and know that your support is there while they are learning at school.

Thank you very much.

Sincerely,

A corner of the room devoted to families positively affects the sense of security and wholeness students feel in the classroom. The children bring their photographs to school with a sense of joy and acceptance. The teacher hangs each photo as it arrives and reminds the child to thank the family for having shared something so precious.

"Back to School Night"

When the parents of Room 4 arrived a few weeks later at "Back to School Night," they were immediately attracted to the photographs. They engaged in conversation with other parents. "Oh this must be you, whose parent are you?" Lots of friendly smiles were exchanged, showing an initial gesture of inclusion and acceptance. The parents were open to hear more. The teacher appeared to be sincere and said she wanted their presence. She told them that they were also teachers and that they had "graduated from the university of life" (Ada, 1988). The teacher also said she wanted and needed their help. Perhaps they in fact had an important role to play, and perhaps those deep wounds they still felt from their own childhood when in some way they thought they were excluded would begin to disappear. Maybe the wounds that were inflicted on their own parents would begin to be healed during the collaborative process planned for the year. Perhaps they should give this school a chance. If nothing else, at least they could give this teacher the benefit of the doubt.

The teacher explained to the parents some of the class curriculum and told them that she had very high expectations for their children. She also told them that she loved working with children and that she thought all children were not only smart and could learn anything but that they were also all artists. She told the parents that all the children in the class would become authors by writing and illustrating their own books and that with many of these books they would be seeking their family's participation or asking for their help. Other books they would be writing together or co-authoring. She hoped that the families, through the book creation process, would share parts of their life experiences, thoughts, and memories with their children and with her.

The teacher then related conversations she had had with other parents over the years who expressed concern about the amount of television their children watched in their homes. The families present agreed that they shared this concern. She suggested that the books they would be working on together would be an opportunity to spend quality time with their children and perhaps replace some of the hours of television.

The teacher confessed that she had written a short book about herself that she was planning to read to the students soon but that she would first like to read it to the parents. It began with an old black and white baby snapshot from her family album and talked about where she was born. There was a beautiful picture of her parents' wedding, alongside a picture of the teacher when she was three, wearing her favorite bathrobe (see Figure 2.1). There was a picture of the teacher as a youngster being lovingly carried by her parents and another with a baby goat named Schwenley whose mother had gone away (Figure 2.2). All the children in the teacher's family loved to feed Schwenley with a baby bottle. The teacher also had included some pictures of her travels to Latin America before she became a teacher and mother. Finally, there were pictures of her husband, her children, and other children she had taught. When the story was finished, the parents applauded. In the parents' eyes, the teacher was becoming a real human being. Perhaps on a subconscious level they could begin to sense their commonalities. Although the teacher's prescribed role would always command respect, the possibility for collaboration in relation to their child's education was emerging.

Next the teacher asked the parents to help make a list of what they thought would be important for their children to learn during that year. A few parents timidly raised their hands, and the teacher wrote down what they said with their names (in parentheses) on a large piece of chart paper. Included were reading, writing, respect, English, and getting along with other children.

FIGURE 2.1

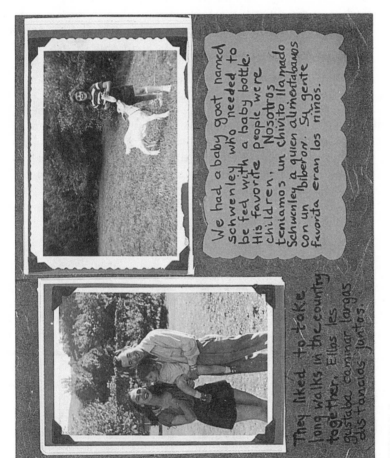

FIGURE 2.2

37

Responding to the urging of the children who were present that evening, the teacher taught the parents a song that the children had been learning and they all sang together. The words were posted on a colorful chart in the front of the room for everyone to see and join in the singing. Everyone was encouraged to have some more dessert and to stay around a little longer.

Since many families still had not left the school building, the principal peeked in to see what was happening in this classroom and to say that the building would be closing in five minutes. The parents were beginning to bond with their child's classroom experience. The next week two Spanish-speaking mothers began coming to the classroom every day. They wanted to offer their help, but they also wanted to learn English alongside the children. They felt comfortable in this classroom and wanted to join their children at school. The teacher welcomed them and also immediately invited them to share responsibility for teaching the students. Because the classroom was organized into small learning groups in different areas of the room, the structure lent itself well to the parents' assuming responsibility. Gradually, the ideas and knowledge of the parents began to interact with those of the teacher and the students within the classroom setting, and they were on their way to a rich interactive year.

Parents as Classroom Participants

Some teachers are apprehensive about having parents in their classrooms because their presence makes them uncomfortable and forces them to be on "display." Part of these feelings are a logical consequence of the unrealistic expectations society places on teachers. Within the traditional paradigm, a teacher should be all-knowing and make no mistakes; an effective teacher is completely organized and has everything "under control." An effective teacher also has all students "on task." Teachers would prefer that parents not see them struggling or not having all the answers.

This attitude is also displayed in relation to other teachers and their peers. As a supervisor of student teachers for a state university, I have found that many fine teachers are unwilling to receive student teachers into their classrooms. Sometimes the reason is that they have just moved up or down a grade level from the year before and haven't "perfected" the curriculum yet. They can even be resistant to experimenting with the idea that a student-teacher could become a partner and that together they could devise a new curriculum.

Are parents really looking for perfection in a classroom teacher? Probably not. They want their children to be treated kindly and to learn what they are supposed to learn. The majority of ethnic and linguistic minority parents carry automatic respect and admiration for the teacher.

They have sympathy for the difficulty of the job, and they are anxious to lend support if asked. The closest and most collaborative relationships that I have seen between teachers and families are those in which the coming together is on a human level of mutual respect and a sharing of knowledge and vulnerability. Parents are sought after as resources and are welcomed into the classroom. Classrooms reflect the home culture and language, and through investigation and study there is a constant flow of information from the school to the home and community and back again.

When this give and take is not allowed to develop, it is often because the parties involved have separated themselves into roles of power and subordination. Teachers are limited by the institutions in which they work. Because they are not generally treated like "empowered intellectuals" (Giroux, 1990b), the need to retain some domain of self-respect and ultimately power is misplaced. Unfortunately, the students and families become the recipients of the teacher's growing frustration and humiliation.

As you continue to read this book, you will have an opportunity to discover your own ways to approach this critical relationship and to explore some of your own fears of engaging in this kind of collaborative work. This work is deeply enmeshed within the philosophy of transformative education. Together, students, teachers, families, and communities are exploring the realities of their present life situations, memories, and knowledge and are participating in critical reflection about this reality.

chapter 3

Home and School Partnerships within a Transformative Education Context

Most educators today accept the general assumption that the relationship between the student's home and school is important. This book proposes that the responsibility to initiate and to nurture this relationship needs to be placed primarily on the classroom teacher as the individual most capable of achieving this relationship in a natural and authentic way. This home and school partnership is integral to a philosophy of transformative education and can best be promoted within that framework.

The following guide presents the basic philosophical tenets that need to be considered under the umbrella of transformative education. Each point is presented with a broader discussion to follow. Finally, the interplay of these concepts is explored through examples of experiences and activities. Teachers may use these examples to begin to build partnerships with the homes and communities of their students.

MAJOR CONCEPTS OF TRANSFORMATIVE EDUCATION

1. Teaching and Learning Occur in a Sociohistorical Context

Students are part of a cultural and linguistic reality and all knowledge that is brought to school is valued. Educators recognize that teaching, learning, and knowledge are enmeshed in social and historical contexts.

Students in our classrooms have diverse cultural and linguistic backgrounds. In many cases, their families are recent immigrants to this country, whereas other students belong to families or cultural groups that have been here for generations such as African, Native, and Mexican Americans. Some came by choice, but many others, either by starvation or political violence, were forced to flee their homeland. Many maintain strong cultural traditions and continue to use their native language in daily life, while others, owing to the social pressures around them or their children's inevitable contacts with school life, have adopted the English language to the exclusion of their own native language. Yet many of these families experiencing the sadness of losing their native language often insist that their children now speak only their native language at home.

Whatever language and cultural habits are found in the family and community, a great deal of information and knowledge can be gained from these traditions, experiences, and distinctive uses of language. The historical or social events that bring such families to an area and the stories that they remember, tell, and retell to their children and friends are cultural treasures that, despite any pain they involve, merit exploration, sharing, and even literary exposition. As Giroux (1990b) states, the students and their families are the "bearers of dangerous memories." Those memories and experiences should frame the core for the students' development of literacy and for all their further learning and active participation in the classroom. This is the key to the community's potential and direction for fulfilling lives.

To help build the kind of self-esteem that is necessary not only for classroom learning but also for all further learning, teachers must accept the cultural, linguistic, and historical experiences that students bring to the classroom, thereby allowing students' to feel that their identities are validated. All knowledge that students bring to school and all knowledge shared by students, including their family and cultural histories, is to be valued. The teacher's role is to communicate an interest and willingness to incorporate the student's total reality into the classroom medium for learning. The teacher in turn must also be willing to share her or his own life with the students and their families. Teachers may do so by recounting personal anecdotes, having members of their family visit the classroom, or sharing favorite books.

2. Education Takes Place within the Context of a Community

As schools help define and take on community goals, teachers come to know and be active in the community in which they teach.

Ideally, education should integrate the values and aspirations of the community in which the school is located. Who is the community? Who are its participating members? The community is the children, the families of the children, people who work in the area and interact in multiple ways with the families; people who create art and make music, and keep the neighborhoods vibrating, the people who live and care and touch the lives of those around them; the child-care providers who wait for the children to come home from school while their parents are at work; the retired and unemployed adults who watch out for the children's safety through their parted venetian blinds.

Education takes place within the community context. The community is invited and welcomed into the school as a valuable resource for knowledge, and as a resource to be worked with, studied, discussed, and understood. Communities are dynamic, which means that they are always changing as they continue to survive. Students can go out into their community and through observation, dialogue, and writing come to understand it better. How does it function, what are its strengths, and in what ways is it crying out for new ideas, new energy, and change? The walls between the school and the community need to come down. Learning, too, is a dynamic process and both will take place in both directions. It is through the students that information both enters and leaves the school. This ongoing interaction leads to the construction of new meanings, and ultimately to the creation of new kinds of knowledge and understandings.

Not all teachers live in the immediate community in which they teach, sharing in its life and struggles. Nonetheless, all teachers, resident and nonresident alike, must dedicate themselves to knowing and joining with this community. They must come to know the people and to explore their resources, for without this knowledge and ability they cannot help their students to know and love themselves. Those teachers who are able to integrate themselves into the community in which they work are more likely to bond with their students. As we come to know each other better, and when the "other" is no longer a stranger, we are capable of greater love. Teachers who are capable of loving their students and their families are better equipped to teach them. Teaching becomes more closely integrated with the real-life issues of the students and infused with caring and sharing. The learning process thus becomes more collaborative.

3. Teaching Begins with Student Knowledge

People are always learning, and thus teaching starts with student knowledge. Teachers are encouraged to develop new curricula with students. Students are encouraged to ask important questions.

As teachers begin a new area or unit of study, they might first explore what knowledge the students already bring to the subject. They might ask: "What do we all know about this topic? What is our collective knowledge? Where and how did we acquire this knowledge?" Teachers should help students to see that human beings, including the students themselves, are learning all the time; and that all of our life experiences and the people with whom we live, play, and work have an intellectual or emotional impact on us. Teachers must also help students recognize the value of the knowledge they already possess and that not all knowledge is gained through books and formal schooling. As students evaluate what they already know, they begin to discover what they still need and want to find out. What are the new questions to be asked, and how will the new knowledge be gathered or re-created? The available textbooks and district curriculum frameworks may not be the resources that the learners will be seeking.

Research conducted by the Institute for Education in Transformation in 1992 found that many students, particularly after fifth grade, feel that the information they are asked to learn and memorize in their classes is often irrelevant and unconnected to their lives. Young children in the Institute study spoke with considerable excitement about learning, whereas in contrast, older students focused on boredom. "Descriptions of the most boring, least relevant school activities suggest that the more standardized the curriculum, text and assignments, the more disengaged the students" (p. 32).

Through this process of validation, reflection, and inquiry, teachers and their students can begin to build their own curriculum or thematic study units together. This endeavor will require library research skills, knowledge of interviewing techniques, and the use of human resources. The creation of new knowledge will become a give-and-take process, generated among students, teachers, and community.

4. Skills and Voices Develop out of a Need to Know and Act

Learning takes place most readily when students realize they have a need to know or to do something that is important to them.

When literacy is developed as part of an authentic learning situation, students have greater motivation to learn and to attain skills. Students spontaneously begin to recognize their need for explicit knowledge in order to get from *A* to *B*. The acquisition and sharing of knowledge can impel them to new learning, and that is why classrooms that are conducted on a cooperative basis are more effective as learning communities. Human beings possess a strong need to communicate with each other. Students in particular need to know how to share information and how to work together to solve problems and to move beyond difficult or painful situations in their lives. In our increasingly global environment, the teacher's failure to teach the skills of working together cooperatively is ultimately a disservice to the student's future.

When human beings are deeply affected by an event or a personal experience in which they have been treated unjustly, voices that may have been suppressed move from silence to speech. By listening to their students' voices, educators discover what their students consider important and what they need and want to know to attain competence, success, and fulfillment. Educators who listen will begin to observe students who are more motivated and ready for collaborative learning.

As a teacher, I must first slow down in order to acknowledge the voices of my students—to take these moments to give value to what is being said no matter how loud or soft, gentle or angry, relevant or irrelevant it may seem. (Institute for Education in Transformation, 1992, elementary teacher, p. 30)

5. Teaching and Learning Are Both Individual and Collaborative Processes

People learn both individually and collaboratively, and the interactions with others can be a powerful force for learning. There are always similarities within difference. Multiple worldviews are an important part of the curriculum. Classrooms and schools should be models of democratic living and give students the opportunity to function responsibly in a democratic society.

The classroom should give students the opportunity for both individual and collaborative learning. People need to know that they are personally competent and capable, not only in creating new knowledge but also in resolving difficult academic and personal problems.

Unfortunately, our society has fostered individualism and personal success and competition to the exclusion of meaningful forms of cooperation and collaboration. Most traditional cultures embrace cooperation and group effort both philosophically and spiritually as a means of survival. Recent research indicates that the benefits gleaned from cooperatively structured classrooms outweigh the advantages of more traditionally competitive forms of classroom learning.

As students learn to work cooperatively to solve problems and to generate new forms of knowledge, they are also creating bonds across cultures and languages. They are learning to listen to different points of view and to collaborate toward a common learning and discovery goal. They begin to appreciate the knowledge and effort that each member of the group brings to a task, and they discover that, despite their differences, they have a common bond: the school context of their lives and, more importantly, their humanness.

In this shrinking world where communication among diverse peoples has become more critical than ever before in history, the school has become the most important public institution for socializing and preparing people for existence in a pluralistic society. Few students, especially those in urban school districts, attend schools in homogeneous settings. But this kind of democracy is not sustained by itself; as John Dewey reminds us, democracy is a way of life for which we must continually struggle and which we must continually reinvent.

Ideally, schools should exist as microcosms of the world in which students can learn, live, and practice democratic principles. Unfortunately, few schools have made this kind of educational experience a priority. Classroom teachers, on the other hand, must be able to create a democratic community of learners in which everyone's voice is heard and in which governing and responsibility are shared so that all have equal opportunity to learn and to participate. We must think about educating all of our students not just to be good citizens but ultimately to govern (Giroux, 1989).

6. Teaching and Learning Are Transformative Processes

Knowledge is critiqued from social and personal perspectives, with an emphasis on taking action. What is becomes what ought to be.

For educators, the 500-year celebration of the discovery of America by Columbus was an occasion to take a fresh look at a body of information that had been virtually accepted for 500 years as the truth. Had the Americas really been discovered by one European man? Who and what was actually there when he arrived? Did he have the right to claim the land for a king and queen? How is it possible to claim something that is not yours? Why did he begin to enslave the inhabitants and initiate a process of virtual genocide? (For an excellent discussion of this topic, see *Rethinking Columbus*, 1992.)

How has the acceptance of myths surrounding Columbus's voyage affected the lives of indigenous people in the United States and other countries? How has the teaching of these myths manipulated the psyches of students over time? How can we begin to know this history and explain it from other perspectives?

Education must provide students with the opportunity to view issues in history such as, "the discovery of America" from multiple perspectives. A story written from a single point of view simply can no longer be accepted as the only truth. Students must be able to critique the knowledge that has been handed down to them and use that knowledge to take constructive action in their own lives to right any injustice that may exist and improve the lives of the many.

Families and communities can be involved in this learning process at every step of the way as the students and the teacher reach out by also taking the knowledge that exists beyond the schoolhouse doors. As families are invited to share their own values and life goals with their children, the children acquire a clearer understanding of what is important to their community and what is expected from them as students, as adults, and as human beings. In this way, important survival traditions will be passed down and kept alive. Teachers and students together can incorporate these goals into the classroom discussion and learning. Models for a democratic society begin in the classroom, and diverse perspectives and voices all find their place.

Members of the community should be welcomed into the school to talk about how they are working to support change. Students can be inspired to work with adults and begin to take responsibility in the community outside of the school.

BEGINNING THE PROCESS OF TRANSFORMATIVE EDUCATION

I want to invite you to look at these six broad philosophical principles of transformative education in relation to what you are already doing in your classrooms. As a classroom teacher, as I began to think differently, the focus of my energy also began to change. The students themselves, their families and the community, became the center of classroom life. I interweaved the preestablished district curriculum around my new central focus rather than allowing it to dominate.

On my first day of teaching, a school service aide wheeled a heavy cart of voluminous books into my classroom. They were five teacher's manuals for reading, mathematics, science, social studies, and music. After looking through each one of them, I decided that there was no way any teacher could cram all that knowledge into their students' minds in just one school year. Later, with some experience and as I grew wiser, I realized that the succinct list carried on the last page in each manual stated everything the students were supposed to know by the end of the year. My recommendation to you as teachers is to look at the convenient lists at the back of such manuals and think about how you might move toward achieving *some* of those goals in your own way. Your own way will be constantly changing as mine has over the years.

chapter 4

Dialogue and Co-authorship of Books

PREMISES

As I began to realize the importance of the home and school relationship and to place this relationship in the context of a transformative or critical pedagogy, I started to experiment and to share my ideas with others. In the remainder of this book, I will focus on developing these relationships through dialogue and family co-authorship of books. I will also discuss participatory research as a way to approach the dialogues, after which I will share my own research work conducted with students and their families. This research includes dialogues with parents and the books that were written by the students and their families (co-authorship) as an outgrowth of the dialogues.

"Telling Our Stories"—Transforming Our Lives

The rationale behind families' co-authoring their own books is found within the context of transformative education. When human beings are presented with the possibility of writing about their world in the way they see it and describe their experiences as they live them, they become more involved in their own learning and are better equipped to transform their own lives.

I began to explore the co-authorship of books between students and their families as a secondary tool to help parents and students in their "coming to voice" (Hooks, 1989). The creation of books became an outlet for recounting experiences and documenting memories, ideas, reflections, and dreams for the future. The process of co-authorship provides literate occasions for parents and students to work together, in partnership with the school, in order to create a personal text that will also be essential in the early reading process.

Validating Home Culture

Ada (1990) believes that because books and those who write them are held in great esteem in our highly literate society the school has the responsibility to foster the authorship of books by children and parents. By neglecting this function, educators may be contributing to the disenfranchisement of the home culture, because the focus of school literacy is on books. Frequently, the books students read at school are about people who are not like them and therefore neither support nor validate their own identities.

Young children who come from families that are not part of the dominant culture face many contradictions as they enter school, especially language and cultural differences, learning styles, behavioral expectations, and forms of knowledge and history that are not their own. Frequently, the students do not have a clear picture of where and how they themselves fit into the school experience. Jim Cummins, in *Empowering Minority Students* (1989), has pointed to this kind of alienation as a major factor in school failure and dropout. He believes that the collaboration between teachers and parents is unlikely to be successful unless the power structure itself is being challenged. Parents need to move from a position of subordination to become full participants in an educational process that incorporates their linguistic and cultural perspectives. Through co-authorship, families build on this collaboration and invite equal contribution to the classroom text for learning.

Families as Protagonists of Their Own Stories

The time parents spend with their children in an enjoyable literacy activity can reap unparalleled benefits. Tizard, Schofield, and Hewison (1982), for example, found that low-achieving children who read aloud to their own parents, even if the parents themselves are not strong readers, thereby derive greater benefit in their reading than when they get extra instruction from a highly competent specialist.

Similarly, encouraging parents to co-author books with their children not only provides an opportunity for parents to engage in literacy activities together but also creates a possible alternative text for use in emergent literacy. Once again, in the words of Ada, children and their families will become the "protagonists" of their own stories (1990). As families become authors, they begin to see themselves appearing in the text. An integration of home, community, and school will become evident as the new texts take on an important role in the life of the family and of the school. These texts can provide the springboard for new learning.

Valuing Diversity and Multicultural Richness

Throughout this volume, I emphasize the importance of a classroom curriculum that reflects the diversity of the students as well as the multicultural richness of the United States and the world. Although some school and district curricula are beginning to reflect this growing multicultural consciousness, the classroom teacher is most responsible for transforming the quality and content of education. The writing of books should be viewed neither as an exercise in curriculum development nor as a "cute" activity to be done with parents when there's extra time. On the contrary, this is serious, powerful, and extremely rewarding work. It must be based on the teacher's sincere belief that students, families, and communities are an important resource for learning and growth and that families and communities can and should be equal contributors in the educative process.

Many parents of our students have had limited years of formal schooling, negative educational experiences of their own, or are themselves products of a racist educational system that has excluded and discouraged them, while destroying their own self-esteem. It is natural for parents to project those memories onto their children.

Those whose first language is not English have often been ignored by schools or pushed aside when they did not understand, only to give up advocating for their child.

THE PROCESS: A BRIEF OVERVIEW

The actual book development process may be conducted in numerous ways. It can focus on a specific theme such as favorite songs and nursery rhymes from childhood, friendship, or frightening experiences. Other books may be created with story lines and may include beginnings, middles, and endings. Teachers may send home questionnaires that can serve as the focal point for a book, or the book may emerge independently with an open-ended format. The artistic element comes into play when drawings, photographs, and methods of binding take on additional importance.

Although the words of the families are of primary interest in this project, I have discovered that the aesthetic outcome of the book is also important. It can raise the participants' self-esteem and motivate them to place a higher value on their own printed words. Computer technology can be made available for writing or transcribing in many schools. Some schools have even received funds for family take-home computer programs.

Recently, Valerie Andriola Balderas, a teacher in Sacramento, California, worked with newly arrived Hmong families to write their own stories with the help of computers. The Hmong people were living as agriculturists in the highlands of Vietnam and Laos and in the mid-1970s, after the Vietnam War, many came to the United States. They have remained identifiable as Hmong because they have maintained their own language, customs, beliefs, costume, and ways of life. Scanner technology allowed the students to incorporate cherished family photographs which they kept with them throughout their journey to America. Balderas helped the families to transfer their stories onto a videotape that printed their words in English as their voices were superimposed in their primary language, Hmong. The children, who were just beginning to learn English, served as interpreters for the adults. The experience of becoming the authors of their own books was powerful. For the students, it provided strong motivation for them to continue to develop their literacy skills; for the families, it allowed them to see that their lived experience as refugees and their cultural knowledge would hold a place of value in the school curriculum.

The program brought together three generations of family members which is an unusual occurrence in American society. The media tend to emphasize the separation of age groups and to focus on peer relationships. In addition, certain ethnic groups are either nonexistent or negatively portrayed in the media. In the writing of one's own book, the student and the family are creating a portrait of their own identities and in this way are building the child's self-concept and sense of place within school.

BENEFITS

A number of rewarding achievements may be attained through the co-authorship of books. In this section let me briefly describe some possibilities.

1. *Co-authorship produces increased communication, dialogue, and sharing within the family and community.* As students begin to ask questions at home relating to their school research, the possi-

bility of ongoing family communication increases. A student may want to know her mother's opinion about a particular topic as it relates to her life's experience. Perhaps she has devised a questionnaire and is conducting an interview with the assistance of a tape recorder. The student asks members of the family and community to share knowledge which she can bring back to school as part of a cooperative project or as a section for a book she is writing.

2. *Students and family discover their voices are heard.* For many students and their families, this will be the first time that anyone has ever asked for their opinion or contributions of knowledge. It may allow many years of silence to be broken. When conversations are turned into written texts, speakers are often astonished by how much they have to say and, in many cases, by how articulate or poetic they can be. Many adults take the dialogues quite seriously because they know that they are contributing to the education of the students, whom they see as the hope for the future.

3. *Personal histories are validated.* This allows everyone's voice and history to emerge. Stories that have never been told, histories that have never seemed important enough to write down, become known and are brought to the classroom as an important component of the classroom text. Each person's perspective becomes essential for the completion of the whole story.

4. *Self-identity and self-esteem are strengthened.* As the voices are heard, and words and histories become important through the validation they receive, people reevaluate themselves in a new and positive light. "I am someone. I have an important story to tell. Others are interested in what I have to say." Students are positively affected when they recognize that their own parents have knowledge and are teachers. It affirms who they are and brings them closer to the roots that have nourished them.

5. *Through reflection, parents relive their childhood and discover the inner child that has been buried for self-protection and survival.* When adults are asked to remember and reflect on their early experiences, they can identify more strongly with their children and become more sensitive and understanding guides and parents for them. They can tell their children about both the joyful and painful times in their lives and show their vulnerable side. Children generally love to hear stories about when their own parents were children like themselves.

6. *Through the negotiation of meaning, important life themes emerge and values are transmitted.* Through the process of dialogue and writing, the important life themes of the participants become known. Adults speak about the experiences of joy and struggle and the

knowledge gained in their lives. As they begin to share what is really important to them, their values become clearer. The superficial layers fall away as adults and students achieve new levels of understanding and self-knowledge. Students gain a clearer understanding of the aspirations held up for them by their families and communities.

7. *Children's appreciation and respect for their parents (and vice versa) grow.* As students begin to discover the depth of knowledge and wisdom present in their families and communities, as well as how this knowledge is also validated and appreciated at school, they gain a new respect for their elders and thus for themselves as members of that community. Because their identities are so closely connected, the respect they feel for their parents transfers to feelings of self-respect. Adults also begin to experience a new kind of bonding with the children who now want to hear and want to listen. They feel a renewed desire to transmit their histories and traditions. An intergenerational bonding that opens up the possibility of maintaining cultures emerges anew.

8. *Students become researchers.* By exploring what they already know about a particular topic, formulating questions about what they still want to know, engaging in dialogue, and analyzing their findings, the students become researchers and bring the family and community along with them.

9. *The teacher comes to know the family and community better.* The information that the students bring to school from home and community expands the teacher's knowledge about her students. He becomes more aware of and sensitive to their lives. He can also include their reality in the classroom curriculum and become a more effective advocate for their academic success.

10. *The building blocks for creating the curriculum are laid.* The terms *culturally and linguistically relevant curriculum* and *building on the knowledge that students bring to school* become quite clear as educators begin to engage in a family literacy development process.

11. *Teaching becomes easier.* The development of a curriculum whose focus is on a home and school partnership is intrinsically motivating, and so the teacher does not need to find ways to motivate students. The work is personal and therefore both satisfying and empowering. In order for students to want to learn, in addition to being academically successful they need to feel good about who they are, where they come from, and where they would like to be going. Students who know that their realities and identities are valued at school and also shape an important part of classroom learning do not have the same need to resist or reject school learning as those who feel their identities are being excluded.

Not learning tends to take place when someone has to deal with unavoidable challenges to her or his personal and family loyalties, integrity and identity. In such situations, there are forced choices and no apparent middle ground. To agree to learn from a stranger who does not respect your integrity causes a major loss of self. The only alternative is to not-learn and reject their world. (Kohl, 1992, pp. 1 & 16) *part* 3

TELLING OUR STORIES

chapter 5

Participatory Research

Some understanding of the philosophy and mechanics of participatory research is important in beginning the dialogue process and in implementing the creation of books. Through participatory research, I have come to respect and love the groups of parents with whom I do my most important and personally fulfilling work. Teachers should become familiar with this kind of research and begin to incorporate some aspects of the practice into their own work. Its philosophy provides a grounding for the work discussed in this book. Becoming acquainted with the ideas of other educators who integrate this kind of research into their lives will definitely inspire our own work.

WHAT IS PARTICIPATORY RESEARCH?

Ada and Beutel (1991) affirm that "Participatory research is a philosophical and ideological commitment which holds that every human being has the capacity of knowing, of analyzing and reflecting about reality so that she becomes a true agent of action in her own life" (p. 8). Participatory research differs from traditional research in its fundamental approach. By attempting to break down the established power roles between researcher and participants, both agents become co-participants in a dialogue. The researcher, who in this case is the teacher, the students, or both, is inviting the participant to speak or write about and critically reflect on her thoughts. The participants may be other students in the class or members of the family or community. Freire (1970) views this interactive process as establishing the participants as the subjects of their own history and encourages shared control and generation of knowledge. As teachers and students through dialogue, writing, and illustration, establish partnerships of co-researchers with their chosen participants, more meaningful participation in the educational lives of all results. The understanding that emerges through this research process is constructed jointly by researcher and participant. This kind of work is particularly appropriate for students and parents from ethnic and linguistic minority backgrounds because their voices have seldom been heard or documented.

Through participatory research, parents can be invited to engage in dialogue, either by the teacher or by their own children, the students. When family words and experiences are turned into the printed word, the thoughts of the participants are validated. The new knowledge that emerges can subsequently or simultaneously be transformed into action. As families begin to participate in this manner, their feelings of self-esteem increase. Parents begin to realize that their words and experiences merit a valuable place in the education of their children.

Through their participation, parents and community members get a concrete view of how they can contribute to their children's education. They also begin to realize that, by sharing their personal experiences, they can help their children and others to understand new and old ways of viewing the world. In participatory research, dialogues are often conducted in the participants' homes in order to provide an interaction within each participant's own environment. For the students, participating in dialogues within their own homes and communities makes the context more immediately applicable.

Park (1989) places the evolution and need for participatory research in historical perspective. The structure of modern postindustrial societies poses a serious threat to humankind's long-held status as master of its own fate. Throughout the world, disenfranchised people are excluded from thinking, feeling, and acting as the subjects of their own lives. Through participatory research, however, the participants can begin to reflect on their own histories and realities and gain a deeper understanding of their strengths and problems. As they begin to verbalize these experiences to the researchers (the teacher and the students) and to listen to their own words, they create a new level of knowledge and understanding that allows them to act and perhaps to change certain aspects of their lives. The explicit aim of participatory research is to bring about a "more just society in which no class of people suffer from the deprivation of the essentials of life, such as food, clothing, shelter and health, and in which all enjoy basic human freedoms and dignity" (Park, 1989, p. 2). Participants begin to see that existing conditions do not necessarily have to continue, but that people can begin to take actions that will transform their lives and realities.

BUILDING HOME–SCHOOL PARTNERSHIPS

Many students we teach in our classrooms have been uprooted and as a result don't feel wholly connected to their new country, culture, or even neighborhood. Most of their families have neither the resources nor the traditional family support systems formerly available to them in their own countries or native communities. In their new lives, they often feel helpless and lacking in personal or group validation. Participatory research invites parents to tap into their internalized and traditional sources of knowledge and wisdom and to begin to feel whole again while contributing to their children's education.

Ada and Beutel (1991) express their appreciation to Freire for his courageous use of the word "love" in relationship to both research and education. As the words of the people are put into a written text, "they gain the prestige of literacy." The written word has the power to make an idea or an experience last forever and become part of history. Ada and Beutel like to think of the words as the "music of our human melody." As students and their families hear the words of others, they feel freer to add their voices to the composition. Students in particular are encouraged to conquer their own fears about engaging in dialogue.

Park (1989) believes that the true purpose of participatory research is to bring together in dialogue those without power and voice and to use their collective intelligence to change their lives. They no longer have to feel victimized as they begin to see the connections between their own lives and those of other disenfranchised people. The students, families, and communities involved in participatory research become involved in a continual life education process that does not end when one project or one book is completed. All participants are psychologically renewed and go away with a strength that will carry them to the next struggle or project.

chapter 6

A Participatory
Research Project
with Parents
of First Graders

THE PROJECT AND ITS GOALS

In this chapter I describe a participatory research project that allowed me to make an in-depth study of the ideas I put forth in this book. Although I was not these students' regular classroom teacher, as a supervisor of the beginning teacher I was frequently in the classroom. The project was carried out primarily with the assistance of the teacher; we believe that the things we discovered together will be of value to any classroom teacher interested in this kind of work. Within the context of a small group of first graders and their families, we began to explore some answers to the major question posed by this book:

> How can educators create a partnership with parents and young students that will nurture literacy and facilitate participation in the schools while celebrating and validating home culture and family concerns and aspirations?

The research was designed to examine this complex issue by following the participatory research methodologies described in the writings and work of Freire (1970), Kieffer (1981), Park (1989), and Ada and Beutel (1991). I invited parents of the first-grade public school children to engage in a dialogue with me about their own childhood experiences with education and the role of their family and community in this educational process. I then asked them to focus on the educational experiences of their own children in school, home, and the community and their involvement in this process. Finally, I encouraged them to formulate their own vision of an ideal home and school interaction or partnership. The dialogues gave the participants an opportunity to speak, to be heard, and to reflect on their own words and experiences. They provided me with wonderful insights into the lives and thoughts of the parents. My hope was that the project could affect the children's school experience by beginning to transform the nature of the parent's own involvement in that process. I conducted the dialogues in the home language of the participants, which was either English or Spanish.

In addition to the dialogues, I attempted to build on the participants' voices through the parents' and children's co-authorship of books. This tool enabled the parents to interact with their children over an extended period of time. The themes for the books came from the thoughts discussed in the initial dialogues. They reflect the participants' own educational experiences, their life concerns, and the literacy practices and activities of the family and community. The books included family photographs and illustrations, and in some cases, they included interviews conducted by the participant with other family members or members of their communities.

THE SETTING

The project must be considered within the social context in which it was carried out. The setting and population may or may not resemble your own school context.

A first-grade Spanish Immersion classroom in a San Francisco public school provided the initial setting. The stated goal of this program model is to raise the academic achievement levels of all students in the program through exposure to two languages. Approximately 43 percent of the students in the school are from Spanish-language dominant homes, and 37 percent of the students are African American. The majority of African American students do not reside in the immediate vicinity of the school but arrive by school bus from other neighborhoods. The percentage of students who score below the 40th percentile is above the district average. Based on last year's test scores, the principal estimates that between 75 and 80 percent of the student population will fall below the 40th percentile.

In this school parents have been virtually uninvolved. It has only a very small Parent Teacher Association (PTA), and parent participation in the classroom is minimal. It is not considered a community school because only a small number of children live within the immediate walking neighborhood. Children are "bussed in" from other areas of San Francisco to comply with district desegregation policies.

THE PROCESS

I invited parents to participate through a letter I sent out to all families via the classroom teacher. Parental desire and ability to participate were the only criteria for selection. I wanted to include parents who represented the ethnic and linguistic composition of the classroom. One of the most important aspects of the project would be the opportunity of an in-depth interaction among the families of different cultural and language groups.

I conducted the dialogues in the homes of the families. As noted earlier, because for many ethnic and linguistic minority parents, the school has not been a welcoming environment, dialogue on their territory provides an opportunity to equalize the perceived power relationships. I felt that this approach would perhaps provide a better opportunity for the parents' voice and knowledge of the family to emerge.

In order to validate the diversity of parent contributions to education, I encouraged parents to speak out on how they saw their roles as educators. I also asked them to reflect on the involvement of the adults around them while they were growing up, and I invited them to begin to explore the possibilities of collaboration with the school experience of their own children. Freire (1973) emphasizes that "dialogue awakens awareness" (p. 125). The process enabled the parents in this study to clarify their understanding of their role in the collaboration between home and school.

Transcription and Sharing of Dialogues

I transcribed the initial dialogues from a cassette recording of the session and then shared the texts with the participants, inviting them to revise or correct any parts that did not represent what they really wanted to express. Each received his or her own printed copy to keep. This step is an essential part of any collaborative effort and also advances the reflective process to a level of greater depth and significance. Upon receiving the text, the participants expressed surprise that they had had so much to say, that it had appeared in print, and especially that their words and thoughts were considered worthy of publication in the creation of new knowledge. This process provides enormous potential for transforming the participant's self-esteem and sense of personal efficacy. In this way, previously disenfranchised or excluded people can see themselves as an actual part of the process where knowledge is constructed and has significance. As the parents themselves develop their own feelings of empowerment, they begin to present a positive new model to their children which can impact the children's academic performance.

Analysis of Generative Themes

During the next stage of the project, I analyzed the texts from the dialogues and extracted the common or "generative themes"—that is, the recurring threads of thought that are woven throughout the dialogues and that signify important issues to the lives of the participants. I used these themes to guide the content of the books that were eventually created by the participants and their children. The subjects of the books were relevant to the participants' lives. Therefore, they were motivated to write their books and to see themselves as the primary characters within their stories.

Family Book Development

The books were actually written and produced during two group sessions held in the children's classroom on two consecutive Sundays and were later continued by individuals in their homes. I found that both the social and private nature of book creation are valid and important. In order for the book project to be an additional tool to record family knowledge, gain voice, and provide a possible connection and support between home and school learning during the emergent literacy stage, it was important that the process remain an open one that would evolve through dialogue and participant input. New themes continued to emerge and were explored through further dialogue and subsequent creation of books.

At the start of the first book development session, I gave the participants and their children a box of supplies to be used during the process. The child's name was printed in large letters on the lid of an attractively covered shoebox which contained items that I hoped would motivate the family's creativity through experimentation. Included in the box were paper, thick and thin markers, colored pencils, crayons, watercolor paints, scissors, stars and stickers, collage scraps, needles and thread, and glue sticks. These boxes were to be taken to the participants' homes at the end of the session.

The first session consisted of an overview of the research project, the creation of a group book, an experience in sewing and binding a simple book, and directions for several projects to be continued at home between group sessions.

The actual list of questions I used to guide my dialogues with the participating parents follows. They were divided into four categories. Not all the questions were asked to all the participants, and they were not necessarily asked in the order shown here. They simply served as a guide. Notice how most of the questions can be interpreted in multiple ways and how the questions are open ended.

In the following chapter, the voices of the parents are presented as they emerged in the dialogues. Also included in Chapter 7 are some of my ongoing reflections on their words.

Questions Used to Guide the Dialogues

What have been the educational experiences of linguistic and ethnic minority parents in formal schooling, out of school, and in conjunction with the school?

1. Talk about your earliest memories of learning. How and what did family members teach you?
2. What kinds of learning took place in the community?
3. Who do you remember as wise people in your family or community? What knowledge did they possess? How did they use or transmit this knowledge to others?
4. Talk about oral traditions in your family or community (songs, stories, chants, and sayings).
5. What did you know about reading before you entered school? How did you learn?
6. What are your earliest memories of school? Did school learning seem similar to or different from the kinds of learning you had participated in previously?
7. How did your school experience make you feel about your home experience? What kinds of comparisons did you make?
8. How would you describe yourself as a student?
9. How do you think you learned to read?
10. What was your family's involvement in your school experience? What were the expectations of the school vis-à-vis parents? In retrospect, do you feel that was an appropriate involvement?

How do parents view their own children's educational experiences in the context of family, community, and school?

1. Talk about the kinds of experiences and activities you have together with your children. What do you like to do together?
2. In what ways do you feel that you teach your children? What and how do they teach you? What important things do you feel it is your responsibility to teach them?
3. What do you feel your children learn from others in the family, and how do they teach them?
4. In what ways does your child's school experience enter your home?

5. What kinds of knowledge do your children gain in their community?
6. Talk about your child's school experience. How would you evaluate it? What is the school providing for your child? How will your child's future life be affected by her present school experience?
7. What differences do you see between school and home learning? In what ways do you see the two merging?

How can educational bridges be built between the home and the school that validate and celebrate the home culture and community?

1. What is your involvement in the school? How have you been invited, approached, or excluded by the school? How do you think teachers and administrators feel about parents? How do they express this feeling?
2. Talk about the ways in which the school reflects or negates what you teach your children at home.
3. Many educators say that "parents and families are the cause of students' school failure." How do you feel about this statement?
4. Do you feel there should be more integration between the home and school life? How do you think this integration could be achieved? What role do you think the school and the parents should play?
5. What are you willing to do? What do you think other parents would be willing to do?
6. Do you think there will be any obstacles? How might you confront these possible obstacles?
7. Do you believe a home and school partnership is possible? Why?

How do parents view the process of family book development personally, in relation to their children's education and in relation to bridges between home and school?

1. What have been your experiences with the book development process both personally and with your child?
2. How will this process be integrated in the development of a home and school partnership?

chapter 7

Dialogues with Parents about Education and Life

In this chapter I would like to share with you the findings of the participatory research project I described in the previous chapter. Brief sketches of each of the five participating parents are included so that you can come to know them and appreciate their stories and insights. The words of the parents are so rich, insightful, and brilliant that I did only minimal editing. Get to know these participants and listen to their stories. I hope their words will inspire you to reach out to the parents of your students in a similar way. As teachers take the time to know the families of the students with whom they work, the possibility for mutual respect and partnership grows.

PARTICIPANTS IN THE DIALOGUES

It was at "Back to School Night" that I made my initial contact with the parents of Room 9. On subsequent visits to the classroom, I was introduced to other parents as Raul, the classroom teacher, told them about my project. Over a period of several months I came to Room 9 on a regular basis to work with the teacher, to sing with the students, and to engage them in art activities.

All five participants whose dialogues appear in this chapter are trying to improve their lives and to provide better opportunities for their children. All have serious financial limitations, and all are either going to school or are interested in getting further education for themselves. These desires are fraught with obstacles. They all do what they think they can to help their child gain access to good education. All question whether they are in fact doing the right thing.

Ena Patricia

Ena Patricia was born and grew up in El Salvador.

> En mi casa no éramos ni pobres ni ricos. Teníamos todo lo que necesitábamos. Mi papá luchaba mucho para darnos buen estudio y que no nos hiciera falta nada.

> [In my house we were neither rich nor poor. We had everything that we needed. My father struggled hard to give us a good education and make sure that we didn't lack for anything.]

Ena remembers that she always did well in school and was given praise and recognition by her teachers.

Ena Patricia is the mother of Elvin and arrived from El Salvador in 1980. She had finished studying to be a nurse. During a time of civil war in her country, she witnessed the disappearance of several of her fellow nursing students. After a traumatic experience of escaping a situation of physical danger, she began to have emotional problems and suffered a stroke that required six months of recovery. Her older sister, who was already living in the United States, helped Ena come to San Francisco. Eventually, Ena's siblings followed.

Since Ena's arrival in San Francisco, she has worked at a variety of restaurant and domestic jobs. She has always felt exploited on her jobs. Several years ago, while cooking in a San Francisco restaurant, she was involved in an accident in which she broke her ankle. After two separate operations, a year of total immobilization, and two years of recuperation, she became very depressed. Her son, Elvin, was one year old when the accident occurred, and Ena feels that her own physical and emotional state became contagious to her son. After her recovery, she studied word processing, but during the five months of searching for work she could only find low-paying jobs in the field. She finally gave up and decided to take whatever work she could that would allow her to pay the rent and support her son.

Cynthia

Cynthia is a 32-year-old African American. She is the only participant in the study who was born in San Francisco. She reports that her grandmother was brought out West as a child when a cousin who was leaving Louisiana asked Cynthia's great grandmother, "'Do you want me to take Shirley with me?' So my mom's mom moved out here with her cousin who basically raised her." Cynthia was brought up by her own mother, who struggled to raise five girls by herself. Two of the girls are mentally handicapped, as a result of their mother's ongoing alcohol problem.

Cynthia was unable to attend our first book development session because her mother had suffered a stroke the night before. She felt the stroke was probably connected to her mother's inability to give up alcohol.

> She's tried it all. I figure if you're gonna stop, you're gonna stop on your own. It's good to have help but it's a mental thing. If you think you want to do something, and you say you can do it, then you can do it, but if you really, mentally, deep down inside, know that you're not going to do it, and you don't want to, then you're not going to do it.

Sometimes Cynthia does not understand her mother because if she gets upset and "gets to talking fast" she speaks Creole. When I asked her if she speaks any Creole herself, she laughed and answered, "No, straight African American."

Cynthia's primary school years were spent in East Palo Alto where she attended schools with all African American students. "I was real quiet. I was the kid that had the books in the hand and went straight to class and didn't talk to anyone. I was a B− C+ average student. No one would notice me unless someone asked, 'Who is the homeliest in the class?'"

Cynthia is now living in a government housing project with her children Christina (first grade) and Kris (fourth grade). She sees living in the project as a temporary situation that will change when she gets her nursing degree and can move to a better neighborhood. She thinks most of the parents there are "bad" and "not caring." "My kids don't play with bad kids. Sometimes I let them look outside the window but it's basically, where I live, drug selling, so they don't play out there. Gun violence and things like that go on naturally." Despite the difficulties in Cynthia's life, she projects a positive, always-move-forward-and-never-give-up attitude about her future and about life in general. Both of Cynthia's children are academically gifted and are top achievers in their classes.

Martha

Martha, one of ten siblings, came alone to the United States from Peru, eight years ago, at 24 years of age. She was the daughter of a career military man, and her childhood years were spent living on a base. She said that the family called the father "el ogro," "el monstruo" [the ogre or the monster]. She had always felt close to her mother.

Friends in Peru gave Martha the names of several people who would be willing to help her to find work. Shortly after her arrival, she became the manager of a motel in northern California. When Martha gave birth to a child, her mother decided to come from Peru and join her in California. A few years later, Martha married an American man with whom she had a second child. After a few years, the husband's developing alcoholism forced their separation. Martha now lives with her two children, her mother, and her mother's husband in a homey apartment in San Francisco's Mission District. The apartment belongs to her mother's husband of five years. Martha is very happy with her living situation and receives a lot of help from the grandparents, who love her kids and treat them very well.

Because Martha's mother takes the major responsibility for the home, Martha feels obligated to work and support her and the children. Although she earned a degree in journalism in Peru, she has never considered applying it in the United States. At the time of this study, Martha was working part time for "Meals on Wheels," a program that brings lunches to senior citizens in their homes. She has also taken and passed an exam to work for the postal system. In addition, she has plans to be trained as a bilingual court reporter. Her having just been given a space for her younger child in a funded childcare center will facilitate these pursuits.

Nosisi

Nosisi was born in Johannesburg, South Africa, and lived there until she was 18 years old. Because of the political situation and her personal involvements, she was forced to leave the country and went to Botswana. When the South African government began entering Botswana and killing the refugees who were there, Nosisi applied to the United States for political asylum. She was sponsored by the Methodist Church. Leaving the rest of her family, a teenage son, and a daughter, and carrying only ten dollars in her pocket, she flew to the United States in March of 1987 with her son Vuyo, who is now in the first grade. Last year, her teenage son was killed by the South African police during a demonstration in Johannesburg.

With the changing political situation in her country, Nosisi wants to return home, but "the reason we are delaying," she says, "is because we need some kind of protection. We are not yet citizens of America. We are permanent residents. When we have our American passports, that will be protection for us to go home." She is active in the South African community in the Bay Area as demonstrated by her involvement in the organization of Nelson Mandela's visit in 1990 after he was released from prison. She does not believe that apartheid has been abolished, even though the newspapers say it's true. She considers herself a pan-African. Even as a black woman in South Africa, she feels that her life was better there than it is here. "My life was very much better because my father worked and was a businessman before I was born. By the time I was born, everything was planned. They had everything in perspective. Life is not as expensive there as it is here. They already had a house. My life was much better when I was under my parents' wing than I am doing on my own." Her family even had servants, although Nosisi says it's difficult to call them servants because they were part of the family.

She finds that living with her child in America presents many personal contradictions. This is not her culture and she doesn't like many things about it, but feels she has to be flexible in raising Vuyo. "Me and him have grown up in two different cultures. I grew up in Africa and he in America. I have lots to learn." Nosisi and Vuyo, for purely financial reasons, live in the same government-subsidized housing project as Cynthia. She sees this as a stepping stone to a better life, but feels that many of the neighbors just remain there and don't try to improve their lives. She keeps to herself and doesn't want the neighbors to know her. "The reason I have never wanted to let people here into my house is because you don't trust. You see the person and they pick up something and go with it, and you are left stranded. We are all suffering here." She feels that once you get involved it means trouble. "People don't sleep here. They are in the streets 24 hours and they know when you're not home."

She doesn't feel that people here care for each other or treat each other like community as she was accustomed to in Africa. "I don't know how to put it . . . words kind of fail me, but it's like people have oriented themselves to me, myself first. People who see your child being beaten up by somebody else will go and look and crowd around instead of calling you. That's not a sign of being a community." She gave another example of how she had recently fainted and fallen on her doorstep. "As part of a community, people would run and check and see what was happening because they know I live alone and Vuyo was out playing. They didn't." She believes it's probably like that in all urban areas of America.

Nosisi has been studying catering and hotel management. She feels that not only are the department and field very racist, but also "if you are a woman in the profession you are never given an opportunity to raise yourself up." She ultimately wants to open a hotel "somewhere" in Africa because she feels she knows the "two worlds," that of the African and that of the tourist.

Henry

Henry is 32 years old and was born and raised in Nicaragua. His family was poor, and he remembers that his parents sacrificed everything for their nine children. During his youth he almost left school until one day, in his own words, he woke up.

Renunciar al colegio es como renunciar a la vida misma, es como renunciar a la educación. Después me fui dando cuenta con el tiempo, que el estudio es la base de la formación de una persona. Es el proyecto de todo ser viviente y todo ser humano para poder llegar a ser algo en la vida.

[To quit school is to give up on life, to give up on education. After a while, I realized that study is the foundation for becoming a person. It is the journey of every human being to become something in their life.]

He arrived in the United States in 1986, and despite a difficult childhood, personal and political problems in his country, and some sadness and regrets about the past, Henry seems to approach everything with determination, self-confidence, and a joyous spirit.

Y que los escalones, por muy altos que sean hay que sobrepasarlos, hay que sobresalirlos y no dejarse llevar siempre por los obstáculos. Si hay que pegar contra la pared no hay que quedarnos allí, hay que seguir siempre adelante.

[And even if the steps are very high, we need to climb over and not let ourselves be stopped by the obstacles. If we bump up against a wall, instead of remaining there we must always continue forward.]

Henry feels that, in his youth, time passed him by and that now he is left with no preparation and no title. "Lo único que me queda decir es que soy Henry y que todo el mundo me conoce por mi nobre." [All that I can say is that I am Henry and everyone knows me by my name.] He felt like he was always postponing the next step in life. "Dejamos que pasara mañana y mañana, nos fueron saliendo los bigotes." [We left everything for tomorrow, and then our moustaches began to grow.]

After the revolution in Nicaragua, the government initiated a national literacy crusade, in which students and young people volunteered to go into the countryside to teach reading and writing. Both Henry and his wife María joined the campaign and that is where they met. Henry participated fully in the reconstruction of his country until he began to feel personal contradictions with the government and the revolutionary process. He spoke about his participation in the literacy crusade and about how getting to know and understand the peasant and his culture helped him to mature and see life's real value.

Creo que fue una experiencia máxima, porque lo hace a uno madurar, le hace a uno ver y entender el campesino, y sus costumbres. Nosotros estamos dedicados a lo que es la ciudad, al movimiento de carros, discotecas, pero en el campo existen personas con gran corazón. Yo aprendí mucho de esa gente. Creo que es más pura, más humilde, más comprensiva, más unida porque nosotros, los que estamos en la ciudad somos hipócritas, y tal vez más ignorantes que ellos.

[I believe that it was an incredible experience, because it forces one to mature and to see and understand the peasants and their customs. In the

city we are so involved in city things like the movement of cars and disco-
theques, but in the countryside people live with generous hearts. I learned
a lot from these people. They are purer, more humble, more understanding
and more united than we are. In the city, we are hypocrites and perhaps
more ignorant than they.]

Henry and María arrived here six years ago with Henry's mother-
in-law, and they are now living in a small apartment with a shared bath-
room down the hall in San Francisco's Mission District. Both Henry and
María are working evening shifts in a shirt printing factory. Henry does
silkscreening and painting of designs on shirts, and María puts on the
labels. They come to school every day both to bring their daughter Jessica and to pick her up. Both Henry and María are always positive and
enthusiastic.

MAJOR GENERATIVE THEMES
EMERGING FROM THE DIALOGUES

Through the dialogues I was looking for answers to three major questions.

1. What have been the educational experiences of linguistic and
    ethnic minority parents in formal schooling, out of school, and
    in conjunction with the school?
2. How do parents view their own children's educational experi-
    ences in the contexts of family, community, and school?
3. How can educational bridges be built between the home and
    the school that validate and celebrate the home culture and
    community?

Educational Experiences of
the Participants

*What have been the educational experiences of linguistic and ethnic minority par-
ents in formal schooling, out of school, and in conjunction with the school?*
The parents' answers to the first question addressed four themes:
(1) the participant's relationship with his or her parents; (2) teaching early
learning skills in the home; (3) passing down heritage, culture, and values; and (4) the family's connection to the school.
Exploration of the participants' childhood experiences through
their memory and reflection provided insight into the past. I believe that
memories stored from childhood, if not recognized and understood, may
carry negative associations and uncritiqued behaviors that can affect
present parental behavior. For many parents, these memories, whether
positive or negative, affect and often determine the kind of relationship
they will establish vis-à-vis their own children's education, both at home
and with the school.

Participants' Relationships with Their Parents

One's relationship with family members carries major importance for individuals as to how they feel about themselves, how they approach their lives, and how they view their options. Participants spoke with love, respect, and admiration for at least one of their parents. The quality of relationships ranged from warm and supportive to cool and distant. At different times in their lives, all received the parental message that education was important. Cynthia appreciated her mother's positive support for her education and the confidence she had in her ability to achieve: "My mother supported me to the utmost! She's there every time I graduated. 'Well my daughter's going to school for nursing and I'm so proud of her' . . . and all this kind of stuff."

Nosisi, whose father died when she was twelve, remembers clearly how he cared not only for the lives of his own children but also for those of the community.

> Daddy was very protective of our family, like any other father. He always fended for us. He was not a fancy dresser but he always wanted to see us look fancy. He was a great public person. Most businessmen looked up to him and came to him for advice. We had a lot of adopted brothers and sisters who my father helped. Parents who couldn't afford to send their children to high schools and universities would come and talk to my father and he would take them to school. They ended up being like sisters and brothers to me. I feel that he was a great and rare person who was trying to build a community though he didn't have all the opportunities with him.

In contrast, Henry spoke about his relationships in the context of the poverty in their lives. He believes that poverty can either bring a family closer together or push them further apart. In his family, it pushed them apart. He did not feel a closeness in his large family.

> Nunca hubo comunicación, nunca nos íbamos a sentar a una mesa, a platicar de nuestros problemas como trabajo o educación. Había solamente pleitos, riñas entre familia, descontentos por nuestras mujeres, por nuestros cuñados y así.
>
> [There was never communication. We never sat down at the table and talked about work and education problems. There were only disputes, arguments among family members, dissatisfactions toward our wives and our in-laws.]

Teaching Early Learning Skills in the Home

In each home parents wanted children to learn the basic skills before entering school. The participants each spoke about a special person who worked with them to teach the alphabet and simple mathematical computations before they entered school. It was usually a drills approach. There would be consequences if the child didn't learn. Martha was slapped on her knuckles with a ruler, and Ena couldn't eat until she learned. For most, the mother was the teacher, but others were taught by an aunt, a cousin, or a retired neighborhood schoolteacher. Cynthia's mom bought simple reading books for her children and made them read together. She remembers,

> She was always buying those little books like, *The Cat in the Hat*. We had an older sister, because I'm next to the baby, so we'd always sit up and just read to each other. That was something you do back in the days when you're poor and couldn't afford a T.V. and mom and them listen to the news; we had to read.

Because of economic hardships in his family's lives, Henry received less, but still he was given some early literacy support from his parents. He knows that they sacrificed for their children and probably did the best they could.

> Lo poco que yo sé, se lo agradezco en mi parte, no digo en su totalidad, a mi padre, y a mi madre el cien por ciento. Ella se sacrificó todo el tiempo por nosotros. Mi padre y mi madre eran pobres. Ellos nos enseñaron poco a poco. Casi nunca tenían tiempo para nosotros. Pasamos el tiempo y yo fui poco a poco aprendiendo a escribir en los rótulos del mercado. Agarraba papel y allí escribía yo y así fui escribiendo poco a poco.

> [The little bit that I know, I thank, although not completely, one hundred percent to my father and my mother. My mother sacrificed all the time for us. My father and mother were poor. They taught us little by little. They hardly ever had time for us. Little by little I learned how to write from the labels in the marketplace. I grabbed a piece of paper on which I wrote and that is how little by little I learned to write.]

This consciousness of the importance of parents giving a head start to their children's education has stayed with all the participants. It is evidenced in the support they are now struggling to provide in their own home.

Passing down Heritage, Culture, and Values

Teaching did not stop with the basic skills. The passing down of heritage and culture was also part of the family learning experience. Important values were transmitted through these teachings, and participants came to know both directly and indirectly what was expected of them as human beings. The teachings included rules and advice about how to live and act, how to treat others, how to be responsible and self-reliant, and the importance of getting an education. Ena remembers that her grandfather's stories were "para que nos formáramos una idea de los tiempos pasados" [so we could get an idea of times gone by].

Nosisi talked about the times in South Africa, when she was small and her aunts and grandparents visited. Not only were their words an important part of her education but also those stories and experiences gave her a sense of identification and connection to her family.

> After dinner we would sit around the coal stove and retell stories. Then one falls asleep and they take you to bed. You learn a lot from those stories because our great grandparents used to tell such practical stories about their lives growing up and what our great, great grandparents did to them. That's part of teaching us and interpreting our culture more simply.

Cynthia reflected back with great interest and fascination to the first time she learned about her family's history in slavery.

> I guess the earliest memories of learning would go back to four or five, on holidays, when we would sit up in the elder's house and my grandmother would just tell us stories that her mother told her from back in slavery days. We were basically learning our heritage. I thought wow, we had a part back in those days!

The value and importance of home was clearly communicated; it was the center of life.

Because Cynthia's mother didn't trust other people, the five girls were kept in the house. Martha was also somewhat confined. She spent her early childhood days playing on the military base, which was her home at the time. There were guards at the gates, and she and her brothers and sisters were not allowed to leave. Their feelings of imprisonment sometimes led to mischievous behavior.

> No podíamos dejar la casa, inmediatemente le avisaban a mi papá. Una vez nos cansamos de estar adentro de la casa sin hacer nada. Movimos todos los muebles, los sacamos al jardín, echamos detergente al piso, tiramos agua, nos pusimos ropas de baño y nos resbalamos por toda la casa.

> [We couldn't go out of the house, or immediately our father would be notified. Once we were so tired of being inside the house without anything to do. We moved all the furniture outside to the garden; we threw detergent on the floor; we dumped water; we put on our bathing suits and slid around the whole house.]

Henry's recollections of his life at home and the nearby community are infused with his mother's teachings and advice.

> Mi mamá me hacía diferenciar las cosas buenas de las malas. Ella decía, "Si la educación no está en su casa, en la calle la vas a encontrar." Así es que respeta las personas mayores y trata de defenderte de las personas que traten de insultarte o agredirte.

[My mother made me distinguish between the good and the bad. She would say, "If there is no education in your house you will find it in the street." That's why you must respect older people, and try to protect yourself from those who will try to insult and attack you.]

Martha's mother gave her daughter a similar warning and advice about the company one keeps. She says that she will always remember what her mother would say when she'd go out with a girlfriend.

Mira esta chica no te conviene. Tú eres una manzana pura y limpia, buena. Si te juntas con una manzana podrida, la manzana limpia se va a contagiar. Si tú no vas con esta manzana, entonces tú vas a estar bien.

[Look, this young woman is not right for you. You are a pure, clean and good apple. If you hook up with a rotten apple, the clean apple will become infected. If you don't go with that apple, then you will be good.]

Martha still believes that her mother's advice was wise and valuable. She sees too many youth going in the wrong direction and letting themselves be negatively influenced. Martha's mother also expressed her desire that her daughter finish secondary school. "Si no la terminas no vas a ser nada en esta país no vas a ser nadie." [If you don't finish secondary school, you won't be anything in this country, you won't be anyone.]

Cynthia reminisced about how family values were introduced when everyone was just sitting together. Believing in God, knowing your heritage, and helping other family members were central concepts for her family.

We would just sit around and say our values. What you are supposed to do and what you are not supposed to do. How you are supposed to treat other people. Always believe in God and raise your kids believing in God. . . . All this kind of stuff. Always tell the kids certain things about the family and about your heritage. Never let your kids forget your heritage and keep on going. As far as our community, everybody helped one another. As long as you have family everybody helps one another. That's what we learned, to help other people. We always went to church on Sundays. It didn't matter if it was storming or lightning, thundering or sunny day.

Nosisi's parents taught her that learning and taking responsibility were the most important attributes.

What my parents stressed most was responsibility. Part of the responsibility was to know who I am, what my culture is, and what is expected of me as a human being. They also stressed responsibility because they were businesspeople and they wanted me to take over the business from them.

In contrast to the other participants, because of the lack of consistent support that Henry received at home as well as the tensions in his family, he realized early in life that he had to take care of himself. "Si quieres progresar vas a progresar solo." [If you want to move forward, you must do it alone.]

Family Connection to the School

Memories of how one's family was connected to the formal schooling process while growing up were vivid. Each of the four women felt their home supported the school, was conscious of the school, and was committed to working with the school. Only Henry was left to his own devices, which he attributed to his family's poverty.

> Casi nunca tenían tiempo para nosotros. Casi nunca iban a nuestros colegios a preguntar por nosotros como íbamos en las clases. Jamás se dieron cuenta si nosotros asistíamos a las clases. Nunca fueron a las reuniones. Constantemente los profesores mandaban a llamar a mi papá, a mi mamá. Pero nunca. Solo matándose, peleándose vivían. Así fué pasando el tiempo y yo fui poco a poco aprendiendo a escribir en los rótulos del mercado.
>
> [They hardly ever had time for us. They hardly ever went to our schools to ask how we were doing. They never noticed whether or not we attended classes. They never went to the meetings. Constantly, the teachers sent notes calling for my father and my mother. But never. They lived killing themselves and fighting. And that is how time passed as I, little by little, learned my writing from the signs in the marketplace.]

For Martha, the school was a place where parents did not take part, nor could they with their responsibility for ten children and a military career. "Eran los hijos y nada más." [It was for children and children alone.] However, her mother went over the homework every night, so that Martha would be prepared for the next day of school. Ena said that when the school asked for help, "Mis padres facilitaron la ayuda siempre. Mi mamá siempre se interesaba en nosotros y ella iba a preguntar por nosotros a la escuela." [My parents were readily called upon to help. My mother always took an interest in us and went to school to ask about us.]

Nosisi's father expressed a strong interest in her schooling, but after he died her mother was not as deeply involved. Nosisi expresses some sadness and regret about her mother's lack of interest.

> My mom was only interested in knowing what grade you were in and what you needed for school. If she had been more involved in my education, as my father was, I would be somebody better off than I am now. Now, I don't look down on myself or feel that I'm incapable of things but I do think that

if my mom had been more involved in our education and less in the business. . . . Sometimes I feel that mom loved us but cared more about the business. That was her life.

Cynthia's mother made her priorities clear.

My mother told us when we were kids that we had to go to school. "If you can get up in the morning and you want to do other things you have to go to school. All I ask out of you is a high school diploma. As long as you make it through all those thirteen years and get that high school diploma." As far as participation, she would go to all those parent meetings but she was not going to go up and say, "Let's have a bake sale everyone!"

Participants' View of Their Own Children's Educational Experiences

How do parents view their own children's educational experiences in the context of family, community, and school?

The second question addressed four main themes: (1) teaching within the context of the family, (2) the participants' relationship and communication with their children, (3) education within the context of the community, and (4) education within the context of the school. All participants felt that education was designed to better their lives and to help them move forward. The word "future" kept appearing in the dialogues. Cynthia believes that if "Kids go to school and learn what they're supposed to learn they'll be prepared for the future." Ena describes this notion as becoming "un hombre del futuro" [a man of the future].

Teaching within the Context of the Family

It became clear that, in their homes, all the participants teach the value of education and communicate this value on a daily basis in both their words and actions. They speak of the importance not only of what one learns in school but also of the totality of being educated by and about life. For all, the support and values transmitted from the home are essential. Henry states,

Yo creo que la principal educación de un niño depende no solamente del colegio. La verdadera educación empieza en la casa, y no solamente de la familia sino que de la comunidad en general.

[I believe that the most important education of a child depends not only on the school. True education begins in the home and comes not only from the family but from the community in general.]

Nosisi daily faces the contradictions of being African and raising a black child in America. At home, she has to make sure that Vuyo is clear about his personal identity. For her, being a mother and having her values known is a constant struggle. It demands flexibility. She uses physical punishment when she feels it is necessary.

> I don't want to say if it's a lie or true but somehow that basic education is from home. If your parents don't care about your life and what you are, it will affect you all the way through life. I want my child to know who he is. He grew up in America and he has the tendency to say, "I'm just black." Well, he's not just black and he has to know where he's from as a black. Me and him have grown up in two different cultures. I grew up in Africa and he in America. I have lots to learn. I am not familiar with most of the ways that parents bring up their kids here. A child is a child. You are the boss of the family and he has to listen to you. The thing of a child answering you back and using bad words and fighting, I don't believe in. I feel like I have the right to discipline my child; I don't call it child abuse. I do a lot of spanking. After a spanking he sort of sits down and listens. Then I say, "I spanked you for this. I didn't just beat you for nothing." I also don't like the competition they have around clothing. I want him to be a person for himself and not because he's competing with another child who has this kind of shoe or that. I don't believe in hot dogs, but I buy them because he loves them. He believes in junk food, which I don't. Somehow I have to be flexible about what I learn from him and how I integrate these things in our lives.

Through her teachings, Nosisi is preparing Vuyo, her first-grade son, to be independent and self-reliant. "You have to share and you have to learn to live with other people because you don't know how long I am going to be here and you don't know who is going to take you over, so you have to learn to be with people." She thinks many American kids are too dependent on their moms, and she is proud of Vuyo's independent capabilities.

> I used to have a job that I started at five o'clock in the morning. I would leave Vuyo asleep in the house, go to work and rush home for him on my break. He will have brushed his teeth, had his breakfast, dressed and be waiting for me to pick him up for school.

For Cynthia, the element of fear and danger in their lives makes her warnings and moral teachings, to some degree, indistinguishable. Her input is essential, and her child's actions reflect the values she transmits.

> I walk out of the house and people are selling drugs without concern about anybody else. I wonder if when my kids go outside there will be a shootout. They should just take all these people away so I won't have to have all these worries about my kids. I feel that if you lead your child in the right direction, hopefully the child will follow your rules and things that you say and go in the right direction. I teach them their morals and values, what they should and shouldn't do. Because the way the world is now you have

to be really strict on your kids. They can't follow behind other kids. What the parent does reflects on the child and their upbringing and what the child does reflects back on how the parent is teaching the child.

Kris, Cynthia's fourth-grade son, who was present during the dialogue session, reiterated what his mom has taught him. "You shouldn't do drugs and you shouldn't do bad in school or talk back to your teacher. Don't be in gangs and set Christmas trees on fire."

In the dialogues, Cynthia frequently criticized what she sees as "bad" parents, parents "who just don't care." She shows very little tolerance for them and feels that they are headed for a life of more problems. She takes her own role as mother very seriously.

> I may have my own personal problems, but once you find out you have kids, you are supposed to put your personal problems aside and deal with the child first or try and equal them off but never neglect that child because you brought that child here and that's part of the future and if you lead that child in the wrong direction, that means that you are going to have a terrible future when that child gets older.

Nosisi again witnesses the same daily problems and dangers as Cynthia but brings a different cultural perspective to this reality. As an African woman, she comments frequently about how she views African American children as being disconnected to any cultural heritage. In her opinion, this presents a serious identity question, which unfortunately manifests itself in negative social behavior.

> I don't exactly want to use the words, "identity problem" because these kids know they are Black or Spanish or White, but they lack something that is not there. What they lack is culture. They think it's cool being in the streets and talking the foul language. Language is part of culture, and behavior is part of a human being. It's part of culture. With these people, one of the things that lacks, down to the nitty gritty of it, is that these people have never had the cultural background. Even if it has been passed down it has never been practiced. It has been just taken like an old fashioned thing. I call some of these young and violent kids in the community who are trying to lead others into this behavior, and I talk to them. I try and tell them who they are and why they should be proud of themselves. There is no need for them to live and die in the project. The project is a stepping stone for low-income people to get themselves together in some way. I think if we have parents who understand themselves and understand the norm of what culture is we could make a difference. These kids are not yet out of our hands. They are still living with us and we could make a difference.

Nosisi told me that she tries to communicate with some of the young people living in her housing project and encourage them to be proud of their identities. She also teaches African dance and poetry at the recreation center which is housed in the project. She sees this as a vehicle for reaching some of the people.

Participants' Relationship and Communication with Their Children

For the participants, the role of parent is twofold. Sometimes it is one of friend and "buddy." The parent enjoys the child's company and friendship and feels that she is learning from her child. At other times, the separate roles of parent and child are clearly defined. The parent is the guide and is responsible for transmitting the teachings, and the child is there to listen, respect, and obey. All the parents spend time with their children, whether it be playing Nintendo, dolls, board games, watching television together, working with the alphabet, writing in a journal, coloring, reading stories, walking to the park, or going out for pizza. All the Latino parents talked about learning many new English words from their children, and the African American and African parents talked about being amazed by their children's knowledge of Spanish. They, too, learn new words from their children in Spanish.

Nosisi, as a single mother in a foreign culture, feels that her son is her closest companion. She finds a great deal of comfort in this relationship. In addition to playing together, they maintain their connection to the homeland by writing letters together.

Like Nosisi, Henry wants to be a real friend to his daughter Jessica. He feels that pushing a child too much can be detrimental.

Martha relies on José Luis, her first-grade son, to be her considerate companion, and as a single mother she often takes him with her to avoid loneliness. She feels that many parents are not real friends to their children and that trust and honesty are important between her and her son.

Ena, like Martha, values the support she receives from her son. She feels that, as his mother, she must teach Elvin right from wrong. It saddens her that she needs to discipline him harshly, but he always forgives her with hugs and kind words.

> Algunas veces la relación entre él y yo se pone un poco triste porque tengo que regañarlo muy fuerte y él se pone un poco triste. En muchas ocasiones, al final del día, él va y me abraza. Un día me dice, "Tú eres una buena maestra." Yo me siento tan enternecida por su cariño. El es el único que va y me abraza. Después de que él tiene tantos problemas conmigo, él es muy noble, no guarda rencor ni nada de eso. Una vez yo estaba llorando y él me dijo, "No mami, no llores. Tú no estás sola. Tú me tiene a mí." Sentí un apoyo de él, y que él se siente un hombre.

> [Sometimes the relationship between us becomes a little sad because I have to scold him so much and he gets sad. Often at the end of the day he gives

me a hug. One day he said to me, "You are a good teacher." I feel so warmed by his love. He is the only person who hugs me. Even after he has so many problems with me, he is so noble, he doesn't hold onto his anger. Once when I was crying, he said to me, "Don't cry, mommy. You are not alone. You have me." I felt the support of a man from him.]

Ena's son Elvin has taught her a lot about life. They are learning from each other. He tells her that she is a good teacher, and he keeps her going. In the dialogue, Ena frequently spoke about the need for parents, including herself, to spend more time with their children. She criticizes herself for not giving her children this time. Within the dialogue, she voiced resolutions to change, for example, by working in the classroom on her day off and helping the teacher.

Me dio ánimo de sobrepasar le experiencia que estaba viviendo y me hacía sentir tan mala. Desde ese día yo empecé a comprender que la vida tiene que sequir y que tenemos que luchar. He visto que no le dedicamos el tiempo que deberíamos dedicar a los hijos que hay veces que sólo les criticamos, los castigamos, pero no nos ponemos a pensar, "Mi hijo me necesita." Yo he visto que necesitamos de comunicarnos más con los hijos para que estos hijos no se salgan de la escuela o usen drogas.

[He inspired me to go beyond the experience that I was living and that was making me feel so bad. Since that day, I began to understand that life has to go on and that we have to struggle. I have realized that we don't spend the time that we should with our children and that sometimes all we do is criticize them, scold them and we don't think, "My child needs me." I see that we need to communicate more with our children so that they don't leave school and use drugs.]

For Cynthia, the only choice is to be a "good mother." For her children, she feels that it's almost a question of survival. Cynthia herself is a survivor and does what she must do. Unlike Henry and Martha, the word "parent" carries less the sense of friendship and more the responsibility for the future.

I try to be a good mother. If I'm not going to be, ain't nobody else going to be. You only get one chance. We sit down to do homework. I do mine also. If they can't do theirs, I'll put mine aside for an hour and we'll just do theirs. I tell them, "It's just something we all have to do if we want to get where we want to be, to graduate and to reach where you want to be in your life. You need to suffer the pain in order to have the pleasure." (Cynthia laughs.) I'm real hard on my kids. I'm stricter than my mom was.

Education within the Community Context

Participants keep a close eye on their children. The streets are not an extension of home, as they were during the childhood of many of the participants. They believe that most of what the children can learn from other children is negative. In front of Nosisi's apartment there is a play structure where children hang out, but she admits that she cannot let Vuyo be outside for a half hour without feeling the need to supervise and to see with whom he is playing. The participants trust their own children but not the environment. The children even return home from school with "malas palabras" (bad words). They have to learn to protect themselves.

An important aspect of the relationship between Nosisi and her son is the maintenance of their culture. Although they live in the project, they maintain their own cultural community. On the weekends, she often takes Vuyo to visit African friends who have children. On holidays, Vuyo dresses in traditional African clothing, and they attend community gatherings together.

She constantly talks to Vuyo about Africa and tells stories of life there. She wants him to know and understand the culture so that he will be prepared to return. Vuyo is impressed and at the same time squeamish about some of his mother's stories, particularly the one about the "cow dung." During one of our dialogue sessions, he urged Nosisi to tell me about the "cow dung."

> What you do is mix fresh cow dung with water and go cement your floor with it. It's like a rubber road but flat and you just decorate it with fresh cow dung and sweep it nice and clean. Most of the families in the countryside cannot afford to cement their floors. We make the designs with our hands and every Saturday we refresh the floor with new cow dung. You can use cow dung for other things, like firewood. We used to take all kinds of cow dung in our barn and mix it with some water because it can be so thick. Just enough to make a kind of dough. You put it together and make it sort of round and put it on top of the rocks and let it dry. You can use that as firewood in the winter when you can't go collecting firewood. It is also very cheap. I tell Vuyo stories when we are sitting at night, just before bedtime. I'm hoping that one of these days, I'm going to take him home, and he has to know these things.

Language is an important element of the participants' relationship and communication with their children. With regard to language use in the home, over the years the Spanish-dominant parents have undergone changes in their own attitudes. At first, they thought it was most important for their children to learn to use English, but their changing consciousness has made them more insistent on the use of Spanish in the family. Ena first spoke to her son Elvin in English, because she didn't want him to feel lost when he entered school. She wanted him to be able to protect himself. As a caring mother, she was doing what she thought would be the best for her child. This caused tension between Ena and Elvin's father.

> Antes yo le hablaba mucho inglés. El papá de él se enojaba porque decía que el niño tiene que aprender la lengua de nosotros. Yo le ayudaba para

cuando él fuera a la escuela no estuviera perdido. Yo le enseñé a decir su nombre, su dirección, y su teléfono en inglés. Yo siempre le hablaba en inglés porque estamos en un país que se habla inglés. Yo lo estaba entrenando y preparando para cuando saliera de casa, él se defendiera, que no se sintiera perdido. Por eso yo no lo miraba mal, pero ahora yo le hablo mucho español en casa porque mi hijo es inteligente y habla perfectamente el inglés y el español.

[Earlier, I used to speak a lot of English. Elvin's father got angry because he said that the child has to learn our language. I was helping him so that when he started school he wouldn't feel lost. I taught him to say his name, his address, and telephone number in English. I would always speak to him in English because we are living in an English-speaking country. I was training and preparing him so that when he left home, he could defend himself and not feel lost. I didn't see this as harmful then, but now I speak a lot of Spanish to him at home because my son is intelligent and speaks both English and Spanish perfectly.]

Nosisi wants Vuyo to speak Zulu with her, but he is very shy and won't speak it among other people. She loves her language and feels that, for her, Zulu communicates strong meanings for which she does not have the same skills in English. It is also another way for them to maintain their culture together.

When we talk our language, you have a lot of idioms which you cannot translate literally to English. We have to put some salt and pepper to make it. Let me give you an example of what I mean by idioms. You come into my house and you mess up everything including my telephone. Then you cuss me out. In my language you would never fight that person but you would say, "When you went to the well you drank the water. You found that water very clear. When you left, you put mud in that water, not thinking that you would return and look for the same well." The idiom tells you what you are supposed and not supposed to do.

Education within the School Context

Positive Aspects.   When participants were asked to talk about how they presently feel about their child's classroom experience, virtually all expressed complete satisfaction. Nosisi feels it's the best year that Vuyo has had so far in school. Martha says that José Luis considers his teacher his friend. Cynthia likes the fact that the classroom uses two languages. Contrasting Christina's experience to her own schooling, she feels that it provides Christina with a broader cultural outlook and also gives her additional language skills for future employment. Cynthia felt, initially, that the pace of school learning today was slower than when she was a student in East Palo Alto. She gave the example of her son who appears to be learning certain mathematical operations at a later time than she herself had learned them. Ultimately, she was pleased and decided, "Maybe now they're doing a much more rounded or broader education and they don't concentrate as heavily on the basic skills. There's more a variety of things now."

In Room 9, the participating classroom for this research, there had been a series of substitutes since the beginning of September. Raul finally arrived as the regular teacher one month into the school year. He spent a weekend reorganizing the room to make it a welcoming environment. Many parents expressed their surprise and appreciation about the changes that had been made. What had been communicated to them was caring and support for their children on the part of the teacher specifically and the educational system in general. Henry described his first reactions to his daughter's new classroom and the sense of honor and pride he felt when the door was opened.

Á mí me impresionó cuando abrió la puerta. El profesor empezó a explicarme. "Este es el lugarcito de la matemática, o éste es el lugarcito de artes, allá tenemos una mini-biblioteca y aquí a éste lado tenemos una marimbita para tocarla cuando están haciendo escándalo para que se callen." "¿De dónde habrá sacado el profesor tantas cosas de la noche a la mañana?" dije yo. Yo me quedé sorprendido en realidad de ver por toda la pared cartelones, y canciones. El viernes que fuimos no había nada, y el lunes que llegamos ya parecía allí. . . . No sé por qué le nace esta preocupacion por nuestros hijos al remodelar todo el salón en esta forma tan sorprendente. Porque, ningún salón que he visto en este pasillo es como el de los niños de nosotros.

[I was quite impressed when the door opened. The teacher began to explain to me. "This is the corner where they do mathematics, this is the art corner, over there we have a little library and this is the little marimba I play to call for quiet when the children are disorderly." I asked myself, "From where did the teacher take all those things from one evening to the next morning?" I continued to be surprised when I saw all the things on the walls, charts and songs. On Friday, when we were at school there was nothing and when we arrived on Monday everything was there. . . . I don't know how this concern to remodel the entire classroom in this amazing manner for our children came to be. Why is no other classroom on this long hallway like the classroom of our children?

Perceived Problems at the School. Although the majority of participants generally felt positive toward their own child's school experience, all, to some degree, noted three problematic areas: (1) lack of control and adequate supervision in the school yard, (2) many problem children in the school, and (3) class size. More long range is their concern about the trend toward school dropout.

1. *School Yard.* Before school, during recess, and at lunch time, large numbers of children gather together on the school yard, as

in most public schools. This is the time when many children get hurt and when fights break out. The classroom teachers are not generally present and are not aware either of what is going on or of what has gone on. Often, when children return to the classroom, teachers need to sort out what has happened and why children are angry, crying, or generally tense. Ena spoke of her dissatisfaction and her own son's accident on the school yard.

Lo único con lo que no estoy contenta es cuando los niños están fuera del salón, que no hay ningún control. Mi hijo quebró su brazo allí.

[The only thing I am not happy about is when the children are out of the classroom and there is no control. My son broke his arm out there.]

Martha feels that the younger children are abused by the older ones and that this creates negative attitudes to coming to school. Both Martha and Ena used the word "control."

En el colegio hay mucho abuso, abuso en el sentido de los más grandes. No hay control. No hay suficientes profesores que controlen a tanto niño. Entonces, los más grandes se aprovechan de los más chiquitos y después no quieren ir al colegio porque saben que van a ir y que los van a empujar, que los van a botar, que les van a quitar algún juguete. Qué sé yo.

[There's a lot of abuse coming from the older children at the school. There is no control. There are not enough teachers to control so many children. So, the bigger ones take advantage of the smaller ones and afterwards they don't want to go to school because they know that they will be pushed, kicked and have their toys taken. I don't know what I think.

At times, Cynthia has taken it upon herself to reprimand children on the school yard and to break up fights.

2. *Problem Children and Class Size.*   Cynthia mentions the large number of problem children and class size. She sees these "problem kids" as taking all the teacher's time.

The only thing that is working against our children is that there are so many problem kids in the school system that the teacher doesn't have time enough for the kids who are doing well. They have this fussing with the kids who are doing bad. If you can get a class with all kids that want to learn then that class will make it. Lower the class size. That's the only thing I can see.

Cynthia offers suggestions and frequently expresses surprise that the schools either can't or don't solve these problems. She also knows that the drug problems are beyond control.

The system is so messed up and the pay is so terrible that they can't get more teachers. The budget. If everything was the way it's supposed to be, a certain number of kids to a certain number of teachers. About 20 kids to a teacher and an assistant. Three bad behavior kids in each class. Now there's an epidemic because more than 50 percent of babies are drug-related babies. If it's not crack then it's heroin. I look at the kids and they look like they are wandering off into space. They don't focus on one particular thing but whatever catches their attention.

Cynthia tries to keep ahead of what is going on at school and advocates the best situation for her own children. She lets Kris know that he needs to be a survivor and that she will accept nothing less than his best.

I've just changed my son into a different classroom because him and Mr. B couldn't communicate good. He's a good kid but now he's in a class with these problem kids. The teacher says, "They just get up out of their seats and most of them are crack babies." I'm saying "what" and the teachers says, "They have problems." I told my son, "*You* don't have any problems so you don't have *no* excuse!"

Cynthia is totally intolerant of other African American parents and children whom she sees as not taking any responsibility for improving their lives. When asked to reflect and come up with solutions to the problems, she offers well-thought-out advice. As a survivor, she concentrates on her own family's survival and doesn't have time to worry about the community or her people in general.

3. *Trend toward Dropping Out.* All participants are aware of the growing dropout trend among ethnic and linguistic minority students. Although this problem does not directly relate to them at the present moment, or to their school in particular, because it is an elementary school, they are aware that it is a question they need to consider. Henry believes that the solution will come from parents, teachers, and students working together but that the adults need to show more interest.

La deserción escolar viene directamente de los alumnos pero los padres más que todo, debemos de interesarnos más y tener más fuerza para enfrentar ese tipo de situaciones pero también creo que depende de los profesores para ayudarles a ellos.

[School dropout comes directly from the students, but as parents more than anyone else, we must take more interest and be more forceful in confronting these types of situations, but also I believe that it depends on the teachers to help them.]

Educational Bridges between Home and School

How can educational bridges be built between the home and the school that validate and celebrate the home culture and community? One of the primary concerns of the project was to hear parent views about how partnerships can be developed between the student's home and school life. Through dialogue, five themes were addressed: (1) homework, (2) parental responsibility, (3) parental involvement at the school site, (4) communication with teachers, and (5) prospects for change.

Homework

Assisting with their children's homework and making sure that it gets done and brought back to school is the most concrete way in which these parents feel they can express their cooperation and responsibility to the school and to their child. It is one school demand with which they can adequately comply. The participating parents take homework very seriously, and many plan their whole afternoon and evening schedules around it. It is built into the home schedules along with eating, playing, and watching television. Both Nosisi and Cynthia believe that whatever is done at school needs to be reinforced by the parent, or it is not learned well. They don't see teaching as solely the teacher's job. Nosisi asserts:

> What is done at school needs to be practiced at home. If a child learns an "A" at school you have to make sure he understands. I feel that when you teach a child something you want feedback. The only feedback you can get is when the children have done it again with the parents and then the teacher can see the progress. It is very important for the parent to know how much the child is progressing in school and also how the parent is doing with the child at home.

Cynthia feels that homework is so important that, if the teacher hasn't given any on a particular day, then the parent should make up her own for the child. That's part of being a "good" mother.

> All the pressure should not be on the teacher. You are supposed to help that child as much as that teacher does. The teacher sends the homework home and the parent has to take it up to make sure that the child does the homework and make sure that the child brings it back to school. The teachers should put more strictness like keeping the child in for recess. The parent should teach the child to sit down and learn. Then she should ask, "What did you learn and do you have any homework?" If they don't have any homework, then make up some homework.

Henry also considers homework a priority.

> Cuando Jessica trae sus tareas, lo primero que le digo es que primero va a comer y después va a hacer la tarea. Si quiere ver la televisión, primero es su tarea y después la televisión.
>
> [When Jessica brings her homework, the first thing that I tell her is she needs to eat and then do her homework. If she wants to watch television, first it's her homework and then television.]

Parental Responsibility

All participants voiced the importance of spending more time with their children, presenting good models for them, and finding out what is going on at school by communicating with the children and keeping in contact with the teacher.

Parental Involvement at the School Site

Several parents thought that volunteering in the classroom or doing jobs around the school was an important way to build a partnership between the home and the school but that personal situations usually make this a difficult option. Raul, the teacher, has been welcoming and has invited parents to participate, but of the five participants, one works full time, two part time, and two both work part time and go to school.

Ena has a late work schedule that allows her to bring Elvin to school and also spend a bit of time in the classroom. She has mentioned several times that she was planning to offer her help a few hours a week, but in reality she arrives, sits and watches, and then leaves. She feels some personal tension being around so many first graders.

> En las mañanas es que estoy allí en mis treinta minutos siempre diario viendo como el maestro actúa con los niños e incluso, a veces le ayudo hasta gritando allí con los niños. Yo he visto que es difícil. Los niños tienen carácter muy fuerte. A veces yo digo, "¡Áy, pobrecito maestro!"

> [In the morning I am there every day for my thirty minutes seeing how the teacher acts with the children. This sometimes includes helping as much as even yelling at the children. I can see that it is difficult. The children have strong personalities. Sometimes I say, "Oh, the poor teacher!"]

The administration has invited Cynthia to become involved in the school in a variety of ways. She once attended a parent seminar to introduce a program in which parents would be learning alongside their children. Although she would like to be more involved at the school site, at present her own education is her most important priority. She feels that the school respects her as a mother.

> I've been asked to join the P.T.A. When I was a kid I never wanted children, and this is new for me because I never knew these things happened as far as schooling and the P.T.A. That was really interesting. I was in it for a while but it interfered with my own schooling. They wanted me to do some more volunteer work at the school to help kids and assist the teacher. Back in June the school wrote a letter asking parents to participate. At that point I wanted to do this because I wasn't sure if I'd be going back to school. I went to the seminar they had. They teach you right along with the kids, and if you don't know something, then you learn at the same time. At the school, they like me because they see that I am into my children's education.

I guess when they see that you are interested and into your child, they look up to that . . . since they say not all parents are interested.

Communication with Teachers

All the participants agreed that both teachers and school administration listened to them. They feel that communication has basically been open and school personnel have been receptive to their concerns. In other schools, this was not always true for them. All felt it was important to maintain frequent communication with the teacher and to know what was going on in the classroom in order to help their children better.

Ena speaks about the importance of collaboration and her personal appreciation of the bilingual nature of the classroom.

> Ayudaría bastante en que los padres colaboremos con los maestros para que juntos con los niños podemos hacer un plan de ayudarle a los niños a aprender. A mí me ha ayudado que el programa es bilingüe y puedo ayudar a mi niño.

> [It would help a lot if we parents would collaborate with the teachers so that together with the children we can make a plan to help them learn. It has helped me a lot that it is a bilingual program and that I can help my own child.]

Martha does not view the present relationship between her home and the school as a "partnership." She believes that she does everything that is asked of her but that this does not necessarily imply "partnership."

> Cuando yo he expresado mis opiniones, me han ayudado pero en realidad, no hay compañerismo. Yo sigo lo que la escuela me manda, lo que la escuela me pide que haga. Es como si yo fuera una alumna también en la escuela.

> [When I have expressed my opinions, they have helped me but in reality, there is no partnership. I follow what the school tells me to do, what the school asks of me. It's as if I were also a student in the school.]

When asked to clarify the statement and to give more details on how she felt about being like "a student in the school," she laughed and didn't have anything further to add.

Although I attempted to encourage deeper levels of reflection during dialogic sessions, I also wanted to remain sensitive to the participant parents by not becoming overly intrusive.

Nosisi maintains that the school reaches out to her and expresses caring and that the actual barriers to communication come from parents, including herself. Twice during the dialogues, she spoke about the need to "come down" to the level of the people one wants to reach or work with.

The mere fact that when something happens at school the teacher or the principal calls or they send a note is a sign of caring. If they didn't care how your child behaves, they wouldn't do that. The parent who doesn't respond or say "thanks" is at fault. If the child has problems, they will recommend a psychologist and this is a sign of caring. I think most teachers do try to meet the level of the parents. The stumbling block is from the parent's side and not from the teacher's side. It is me that has an attitude. The school has tried several times to get me to be involved. I have met with the teacher and told him several times that I would come and help. Now I am working and also in school, so it's hard for me to get into the class.

Cynthia uses the word "future" once again when she speaks about the possibility of a partnership. She believes that it is the parents' responsibility to cultivate the partnership if they care about their child's future.

If the parent and the teacher are working together and that child is still failing, that's that child's fault. If the parent and the teacher are working together, there shouldn't be any problem. If there still is a problem, then that child should be checked. A lot of parents just don't care. They could care and participate. I have a friend whose kids go to the same school, and I tell her she should go see the teacher. She says she doesn't have time for the kids, but I said, "That's part of the future. Deal with it. I deal with mine." It's hard. I don't think a partnership is a reality. If they are good parents and you can get through to them then you can work it out. Then there's a good possibility of a partnership.

Cynthia expresses contempt for both children and parents who "don't care." The blame goes entirely to them. When the researcher asked her if teachers care, she vacillated. She finally concluded, however, that they care less than they used to because there are too many problem children now, and the teachers are underpaid and overworked.

Ena blames herself, once again, for not devoting enough time to her child vis-à-vis his school environment. She believes that parents, in general, are failing in this area.

El único problema que hay es que los padres de familia no tenemos tiempo, o no lo hacemos para eso. Creo que en este punto es que fallamos los padres de familia. Es importante de tener más interés en ayudar al profesor, más que todo y comunicarse con el maestro. Yo creo que los padres tenemos más conocimiento en lo que está pasando en la escuela y en lo que podemos nosotros ayudar en el tiempo libre con los niños.

[The only problem is that parents don't have time, or we don't make time for this. I think that in this area we are failing as parents. It's important to have more interest in helping the teacher, especially in communicating with him. I think that we as parents have more knowledge about what's happening in school and that we can help with the children in our free time.]

The participants place a lot of blame on themselves. In general, they feel that they are ultimately responsible for initiating the home and school partnership and that they have been lax. They do not see their reasons for their lack of involvement as sufficiently important or even valid.

Many of the participants' words appear to be expressions of "internalized oppression" which can frequently lead to self-deprecation and peer deprecation. Similar ways of viewing one's self, peers, and loved ones have frequently been documented in the literature.

> Internalized oppression is this turning upon ourselves, upon our families, and upon our own people, the distress patterns that result from the racism and oppression of the majority society. . . . Anytime I take action or do not take action on the basis of any of these feelings, I am giving in to a pattern of internalized oppression, racism and powerlessness. (Lipsky, 1987, p. 4)

Freire (1970) explains this kind of oppression:

> Self-deprecation is another characteristic of the oppressed, which derives from their internalization of the opinion the oppressors hold of them. So often do they hear that they are good for nothing, know nothing, and are incapable of learning anything, that they are sick, lazy and unproductive, that in the end they become convinced of their own unfitness. (p. 49)

Freire (1970) also discusses the myths that the oppressor has deposited in the minds of the oppressed. The internalization of these myths, which are presented through forms of mass media, are essential to keep the people subjugated and are "indispensable to the preservation of the status quo" (p. 135). Among the myths cited by Freire, which have surfaced in the dialogues during this study and which represent expressions of internalized oppression are: (1) the myth that anyone who is industrious can be an entrepreneur and that the oppressed are simply lazy and dishonest; (2) the myth of the equality of all people; (3) the myth of the oppressor's natural superiority; and (4) the myth of the generosity of the elite.

If these myths are accepted, it follows that parents who do not participate within the school structure are probably lazy. Because every American has access to education and has been provided with equal opportunity, it is one's own fault for not partaking. The teachers and administrators who represent the educational institution are generous and caring people who have reached out to the parents. In addition, they generally know what is best for the students and their families. The dialogues indicated that the participants have internalized many of these assumptions. Further dialogues may have led to a deeper awareness of this issue.

Freire uses the term *conscientizacao* to describe the process of coming to consciousness. Specifically, it refers to "learning to perceive social, political, and economic contradictions, and to take action against the oppressive elements of reality" (Freire, 1970, p. 19). Although in this study the participants and I began to engage in such a learning process, there were inherent limitations on the extent of the inquiry, including the traditional structure of the public schools, the limited time frame of the study, and my status as an outsider to their community.

Nosisi recognized the need to "meet people where they are at," and Henry, while not having read the work of Freire, ultimately would agree that getting to know others well and working together to try to change their lives can be achieved only through dialogue.

Prospects for Change

Through the dialogues, the participants expressed many ideas about why stronger bridges were not being built and how such bridges might begin to be built between the homes of the students and the school. In general, the tone was one of optimism. Henry was critical of the school administration. He felt that it should take a stronger role, perhaps even the lead.

Yo creo que no ha habido suficiente comunicación de la escuela con los hogares. Nosotros sólo recibimos avisos para las juntas. Yo creo que todos tenemos la necesidad de que la dirección establezca más contacto con las familias, invitando los padres a participar más.

[I think that there hasn't been enough communication from the school to the homes. We only receive notices to come to meetings. I feel that we all need the administration to establish more contact with families and invite parents to participate more.]

Ena suggested that changes would begin to occur if parents united and made an effort.

Yo creo que como en cualquiera, siempre existen obstáculos. Pero yo creo que si nos unimos para hacer esto se va a llevar a cabo pero si no hay fuerza, no se hace nada. Si los padres nos tomamos optimismo, lo vamos a llegar a hacer.

[I believe that like anything, obstacles always exist. But I think that if we join together to do this, we will succeed. If there is no effort, nothing happens. If parents are optimistic, we will get there.]

Henry suggested the idea of a "mass meeting" in which all cultural and language groups can come together and express their support for the students.

¡Lo que necesitamos es una reunión en masa! Aquí nosotros hablamos español, allá hablan americano, otros hablan chino, filipino, camboyano, vietnamés . . . una infinidad de lenguas. Quizás una persona que habla inglés puede reflejar el mensaje de todos. O mejor, reunirnos los latinos porque somos el grupo que necesitamos trabajar más. Tenemos un porcentaje de deserción más alto. Entonces, deberíamos reunirnos los latinos no solamente para ayudarles a nuestros hijos sino también a otros alumnos y a protegerlos y a incitarlos a que sigan con sus estudios. Con esto vamos a estar conscientes nosotros de que nos estamos preocupando por ellos. No solamente para nuestros hijos que están creciendo sino para apoyar también a otros padres de familia y que se sientan también apoyados.

[What we need is a mass meeting! Here we speak Spanish, there others speak American, others speak Chinese, Filipino, Cambodian, Vietnamese . . . an infinity of languages. Perhaps one person who speaks English can reflect the message of everybody. Better yet, we the Latinos, because we are the group that needs to work hardest because we have the highest percentage of dropouts, should unite not only to help our own children but other students too. We need to protect them and inspire them to continue with their studies. With these actions, they will become aware of how concerned we are about them. Not only for our own children that are growing up but also to support other parents.]

Henry reformulated this idea as he reflected on the high dropout rate among Latino students. He recommended that before organizing a mass meeting, Latinos perhaps need to struggle hard with each other to resolve their own problems.

Nosisi believes that many parents perhaps do not yet understand why it is important that families "integrate" themselves with the school. Through her work in Africa, she has learned that the way people are approached is important. Above all, they must be approached with respect and an open mind. She suggests that parents also need to talk with one another and to share their knowledge and understanding.

I am very much willing to close the gap between Vuyo's home and school life. Many parents do not understand how these two lives can be brought together. I think that it is up to us parents who understand the importance of this to talk to fellow parents. The only way we can integrate ourselves is among ourselves. When you integrate with people, you have to come down to the level of those people for them to understand you and talk to you. I have been involved with so many groups and taught the children in refugee camps in Botswana that I know that you have to come down to the level of the people. People only learn what is taught when in their mind they feel that you are at their level. I don't care if you are a professor or the president. The main obstacle to learning is thinking that you already know everything and that also you are better than the other person. Education never stops for anybody.

Henry also spoke of the importance of parents beginning to know and talk to one another. Again, without being familiar with Freire's work, he is in agreement as to the value of dialogue.

Nosotros, los padres tenemos que conocernos mejor. Y no solamente a saludarnos cuando nuestros hijos están formados. No solamente decirnos "hola, hola" e irnos despúes cada quien por su lado. . . . Creo que eso nos daría más relación, más comunicación, y todo que termina en "ción."

[We, the parents, must get to know each other better. Not only to greet each other when our children are lining up before school, not only to say, "hello, hello," and afterwards each one leaves and goes her own way. . . . I believe that this will promote more relation, more communication and everything that ends with "tion."]

Henry believes that when parents begin to talk with each other and support each other, the lives of the children will change. Parents' knowledge, derived from real experiences, can translate into advice that they can give to each other.

Quizás una persona que haya tenido una vivencia de este tipo para que ella dé él mensaje de apoyo a otras madres. O sea, que haya tenido la deserción de un hijo en la escuela para que ella ayude a otros padres de familia a que no se cometa el mismo error.

[Perhaps one parent who has lived with the experience of having a child drop out from school can bring the message to other parents so that they will not make the same error.]

Henry thus arrives at an idea that would give all the parents in the community a voice. Together they can write a book for their children, expressing their caring and letting them know that they want to help them realize their life dreams.

Creo que necesitaríamos saber la opinión de todos los padres, para formar un libro verdadero, un libro que ocupe un espacio en la biblioteca. Sería un mini-libro que pueda ser usado en otras escuelas y que lleve un mensaje claro y preciso de la realidad de nosotros los padres y que tenemos la gran intención de la realización de nuestros hijos. Un libro que no solamente muestre nuestras experiencias sino que muestre a nuestros hijos que estamos interesados en ellos y vamos a hacer todo lo posible para que su sueño se convierta en realidad. No vamos a dejar que nuestros niños dejen de soñar, vamos a ayudarles a que mañana cuando sean mayores sus sueños sean verdad. Y esto depende de nosotros.

[I think that we would need to know the opinion of all the parents, to put together a real book that will be placed in the library. It would be a mini-book that would be used in other schools and bring a clear and precise message of the reality of our parents and of their great intention for the success of our children. The book would not only show our experiences but would show our children that we are interested in them and are going to do everything possible to change that dream into a reality. We are not going to allow our children to stop dreaming. We are going to help them so that tomorrow when they are older their dreams will become true. And this depends on us, the parents.]

THE DIALOGUES AS A STARTING POINT

I recorded and transcribed the words of these five parents during two dialogues. I posed a series of questions at the first meeting and after a careful rereading and analysis of the texts returned for a second round of questions designed to clarify or deepen the original thoughts and reflections. The meetings and the family book development all took place over a period of four months. The majority of dialogues were conducted with the participation of the classroom teacher. All the participants were invited to my home at the end of the project to hear about the findings of the study and to share final reflections.

In addition to the dialogues, I held two group book development sessions in the children's classroom on two consecutive Sunday mornings. Together we tried a variety of ways to put together the books, and we also wrote some books collectively. All the parents agreed to complete the book development process, with their children, in their homes. In the next chapter you will have an opportunity to see the books that were created based on the themes that emerged in the dialogues. I also include my analysis and actual illustrations from the books.

chapter 8

Co-authorship of Books Based on Dialogues about Education and Life

EXAMPLES FROM THE
PARTICIPATORY RESEARCH PROJECT

The power of the dialogue conducted through participatory research allows the participants to hear each other and to come to know and appreciate another's experiential perspective. When a teacher takes this step with the parents of her students, it leads to invaluable knowledge for both parties and to mutual trust. This may become a moment of truth for the teacher as she begins to see the necessity of building a learning community based on the reality of the student and family's life.

In this chapter I will present the books as they were actually created in the project by the first-grade students and their parents. In this way, the reader can see how, through dialogue, we can make creative use of real-life themes and concerns for nurturing literacy and facilitating participation in the schools. At the same time, we can celebrate and validate home culture and family concerns and aspirations. I chose the themes for the books based on the participants' common interests and concerns as they emerged from my initial dialogues with them. The following titles were used to identify the books as we were working.

1. Childhood Friendships
2. Families Building Together
3. Families as Problem Solvers through Struggle and Change
4. Families as Protagonists of Their Own Stories
5. Codification Based on Community Life

Although some books were intended to be individually created by one family, others were conceived as a group effort to which each participant would contribute one page in a collective work.

My discussion of each book includes the design and rationale for choosing the particular theme, with examples from the books created within the thematic category, and an analysis of the books created and my own reflections on them.

The goal of the book development component of this project was to provide an additional tool to give voice to parents while offering them the opportunity to engage in literacy development activities with their children. Throughout the process, I continually focused on how the classroom teacher could develop such texts so that they could become an integral part of all classroom learning.

In the four months of the project, although I encountered many difficulties and setbacks, I experienced so many wonderful moments that I was always encouraged to continue. The most notable difficulties were the following:

1. Some participants arrived late to the sessions or did not show up at all.
2. Participants were frequently unreachable by telephone or did not return messages.
3. Family illness, accidents, and unforeseen circumstances commonly occurred among all participants. These included a fall from a ladder, a mother's stroke, a serious flu, a young child's hospitalization for a rare disease, an unexpected pregnancy, and, finally, the contracting of foot-hand-and-mouth disease by a participant's child.
4. One participant's work schedule was changed without notice, making the parent unable to attend the book development session.

In the second dialogue, all the parents, without exception, stated that at least once during the process they had felt good about working with their child or felt proud of what they had produced. These comments were encouraging in themselves, but when shared in the group, they also inspired the other participants and allowed me to continue the process without losing hope. While none of the five participants involved in the book development process actually completed all the books that were introduced, they produced many remarkable insights. The following section includes examples from the five book themes, with at least two samples from each participant.

Theme 1: Childhood Friendships

Design and Rationale

In the first dialogues, when the participants were asked to reflect on their early learning experiences, all spoke about childhood friendships. They described classmates, children with whom they walked to school along country roads, or sibling companions. Later in the dialogues, they expressed concern about the friendships their own children might develop, which might lead them down the wrong path.

When parents share childhood memories with their own children, they are creating the possibility for increased closeness in the relationship. Children enjoy hearing about times when the parent was small and like themselves. They want to know who their parents' friends were and why, and they also are inquisitive about what they liked to do together. When parents take the time to remember and to share those memories, they are also remembering for a moment how it feels to be a child. These memories make parents more responsive to their own children's anxieties and needs. A book about childhood friendships developed in a classroom will give children insight into the qualities of friendship that were important to their parents when they were small. A discussion of the intergenerational similarities and differences may ensue.

I presented the concept of childhood friendships to the participants at the first session and invited everyone to brainstorm what friendship meant to them. These are their words:

The Parents

- *sinceros* [sincere] (Martha)
- *la unión de dos personas con sentimientos comunes, iguales* [the union of two people with mutual feelings, equal] (Henry)
- *sincera, comprender uno al otro* [sincere, mutual understanding] (Ena Patricia)
- talking and understanding (Nosisi)
- someone to confide in, someone you can trust, someone you can go to when you can't go to anyone else (Cynthia)

The Children

- *son bonitos* [they are beautiful]
- you can make friends and play with them
- nice
- come to their house, visit
- *llega a su casa* [go to their house]
- hugging
- someone who shares
- respect

Analysis and Reflections

Ena Patricia's contribution to the book was a description of her best friend, Any (see Fig. 8.1a). She is Ena's younger sister who now shares her apartment in San Francisco. Ena's son Elvin's best friend is his cousin (Fig. 8.1b, p. 102). I was curious about the color Elvin chose in the illustration for his cousin's skin. I asked Ena Patricia to explain. "No, Elvin's cousin is not black but Elvin likes *negritos*" [black children]. Most recently, he asked his mother what color skin his own children would have if he married an African American girl. He has talked to his mother about a little girl in his class whom he likes a lot. Elvin is a curious and physically active child. The teacher told me that Elvin does indeed appear to follow and imitate the actions of the African American children in the classroom. Being in an ethnically and linguistically diverse classroom provides students the daily opportunities to explore their own identities in relation to others. I believe that Elvin's illustration represents an element of this exploration and the reality of his classroom experience.

Henry stated that in thinking about his childhood friend and in sharing the memory, he was able to return to that time in his life and relive it, feeling like a child once again. In his illustration, he also tried to give a sense of the whole environment in drawing the countryside and the well in the back of his house (Fig. 8.2a, p. 103). Meanwhile, his daughter Jessica worked happily and independently at a table opposite him. She wrote about her best friend Stephanie who lives in her apartment house and who is also in the same first-grade classroom in school (Fig. 8.2b, p. 104). Incidentally, Henry was the only participant who neither hovered over nor criticized his child's work. He reflected that same parenting style in the dialogues when he stated that the parent-child relationship should be one of friendship and support.

At the end of the session, as each participant read his or her page aloud, and it was translated into the second language, there was a glow of satisfaction in the room. The researcher's colleague, who was videotaping the session, described it as a "very special moment."

Mi mejor Amiga Es Any.
Y me gustaba jugar a las muñecas.
Siempre Ibamos Ala Escuela Juntas.

[My best friend is Any.
And I liked to play dolls
with her. We always went
to school together.]

Ena Patricia

FIGURE 8.1a

FIGURE 8.1b

Momentos de mi Infancia, detrás, de mi casa, pequeño Llano de aventuras y de grandes alegrías. con mi Mejor amigo. Walter. D.

Uno durante, la infancia, tiene muchos amigos, con quiénes comparten, momentos alegres de la vida, Pero siempre tenemos, uno en especial, él que está con nosotros, en lo bueno y en lo malo. Compartir problemas y ayudarnos a salir de ellos.

Es por eso que compartir, hoy Momentos de nuestra infancia, con nuestros hijos casi. es volver a nacer.

Moments from my childhood behind my house _ a small field for adventure and great fun with my best friend Walter D... Each of us during childhood has many friends with whom we share happy moments; but always there is one special one with whom we share the good and the bad. ... sharing problems and helping each other to get beyond them. That is why to share today childhood moments with our children gives us the opportunity to feel like a child once again.

Henry

FIGURE 8.2a

Estefany y yo somos amigas desde pequeñas, y hemos jugado siempre.

[Stephanie and I have been friends since we were small, and we have always played together.]

Jessica

FIGURE 8.2b

Theme 2: Families Building Together

Design and Rationale

This book was inspired by the participants' expressed desire to engage in enjoyable activities with their children. For the children, these activities most often take the form of playing a Nintendo game or watching television. I wanted to offer the structure of a creative activity that could be enjoyable for the whole family, while at the same time serving as an occasion for literacy development using the voices of the participants and their families.

I gathered together a variety of miniature building blocks with accompanying accessories and put the collection of materials into an old black suitcase and loaned it to each participant in turn. I explained to each participant that I would like them to create a block structure in any way they wished, in partnership with their child and other family members. They could use all or some of the contents of the suitcase. Included in the collection were cars, trains, tracks, furniture, a mirror, farm and jungle animals, a multiracial group of persons, and an assortment of building blocks of different sizes and colors. Participants were asked to discuss and build collectively, and to view the building as a stimulus for writing a story. They were then to take a photograph of the participant builders and writers with the building. All the participants said they possessed a camera and were willing to do this project. Each participant's story and photograph would be placed in a group book.

Analysis and Reflections

I was present when Nosisi and Vuyo made their building and composed their story (Fig. 8.3, p. 106). We were in a restaurant together, and Vuyo had made the building while Nosisi and I were conversing at another table. Together, they narrated the story with ease into a tape recorder. Both took turns developing the narrative sequence, and each accepted the other's contributions. The process was full of natural give and take and pleasure. Nosisi laughed lovingly at Vuyo's humor, and Vuyo listened attentively to Nosisi's wisdom.

The major themes developed through their story were survival, creative struggle to overcome difficult conditions, hope, self-respect, and ultimately triumph. These are ever present themes in the lived reality of Nosisi and Vuyo, political refugees living in a low-income housing project in San Francisco. When presented with the opportunity, this became their inspiration for an oral and written text. Nosisi beamed with parental pride when I commented on the facility and beauty of Vuyo's articulation. For her this was an apparent validation, by someone she respected, of the success of her struggle to raise her child in a foreign culture.

Once upon a time there was a train going across the bridge. The cars had stopped because there were no more tracks. Everybody looked at the train and everybody got excited. And so everybody got off the train because there were no more tracks.

They took off the furniture from the train and then they sat down. There was a bath. There was a chair, sofas, a rocking chair and a fireplace. Everybody kind of made themselves comfortable. They kind of made a home near the train track and the bridge. They forgot their chairs, so somebody went back and got the chairs. They had something covering their house. They made a house by themselves so they put their furniture in.

They were living in America. They had to farm around and look for ground because there were no jobs around. They started farming and fishing. They went hunting animals and they went for walks. They saw a skeleton and a tiger fighting. The skeleton flew and then got eaten. So they ran from him to catch a shark to eat it. That was what they did everyday; go hunting in the forest, and fishing. They saw sharks around all the time. That's what they ate most of the time; fish and wild animals. They would have to learn to plant vegetables or they would have to eat roots from the forest.

One elephant snuck into the house and he thought he saw another elephant but it was himself. He broke the mirror. He did everything wild. They just sat around the house and hunted and hunted and talked.

Finally, they got a whole bunch of money and bought a whole bunch of food so they didn't suffer. They finally made means. They exported their fish because they had so much. They traded their fish with other villages around and with their crops they made a lot of money. They could take themselves out of the train tracks and in the end try to build themselves a better home. They even made a new train track.

FIGURE 8.3

Theme 3: Families as Problem Solvers through Struggle and Change

Design and Rationale

Many parents of children in urban public schools have had only limited formal schooling, but this does not mean, as educators sometimes believe, that they have not experienced many challenges and struggles in their lives. Although such struggles are rarely sought after or planned,

Luchar por lo que uno ama.
Cuando tuve mi primer hijo,
Jose Luis tuve que cambiar
por su bien y por su
felicidad. Ser más, responsable.
[Struggle for what one loves ... when José Luis, my first
child was born, I had to change my own life for his well
being and happiness ... to be more responsible.]

FIGURE 8.4a

they nevertheless are aspects of life that need to be resolved or overcome. Most human beings have learned to deal with the challenges they encounter and as a result may often make major changes in their lives or situations. One may or may not have a choice in the struggle toward a specific end.

All parents are by nature problem solvers and while coming up with solutions weave many pieces of information together and reflect on them before making a decision. Children need to experience their parents as problem solvers. They need to hear about their struggles and to find

Sometimes when my friend is mean I don't want to play with him.

FIGURE 8.4b

out what knowledge and reasoning process their parents used to solve a problem. In this way, they can gain greater admiration and respect for their parents, even though their parents had little formal schooling. During my dialogues with the participants, all of them described how they have struggled during their lives and continue to struggle in the present.

Classroom teachers can help foster feelings of admiration and respect in their students by promoting activities such as book development in which parents can share their experiences. Some projects will require

FIGURE 8.5a

parental responses such as questionnaires in which childhood memories or family knowledge are shared. As responses are returned to school, teachers can express positive interest and use those responses for classroom discussion and analysis.

During the second book development session, I asked the participants to describe what the word "struggle" meant to them. I then asked them to recall a time in their lives, recent or past, when they had to struggle to solve a problem or to bring about a desired change or transformation. Parents and children worked side by side.

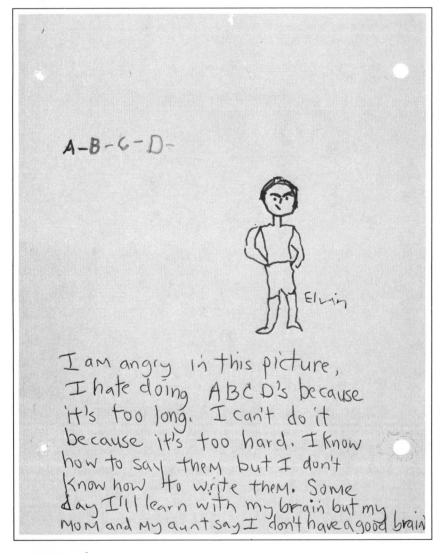

A-B-C-D-

Elvin

I am angry in this picture,
I hate doing ABCD's because
it's too long. I can't do it
because it's too hard. I know
how to say them but I don't
know how to write them. Some
day I'll learn with my brain but my
mom and my aunt say I don't have a good brain

FIGURE 8.5b

Analysis and Reflections

Through both her drawing and words, Martha communicated that she had had to fight for what she loved (Fig. 8.4a, p. 107). The birth of her first child mandated new responsibilities. As all mothers soon discover, it involved changing her own life to adapt to the needs of another person, to consider his happiness and well-being above her own.

FIGURE 8.6a

The dialogues clearly show that being a mother is very difficult for Martha. Although previously she did not see herself as a warm or loving person, she is gratified that her children have nourished this quality, because she can't avoid their unconditional love. Holding a job to support them is also difficult for Martha. She is constantly thankful for the help and support she receives from her mother, who lives with them. Her mother's presence has made survival a bit easier.

FIGURE 8.6b

In contrast, the other three women participants did not have their mother's support in raising their children. Ena Patricia has the support of her sister, Nosisi has no one from her family living in this country, and Cynthia has sisters and her mother who pitch in occasionally. Henry lives with his wife, María, and his mother-in-law.

José Luis, Martha's son, seemed to focus on the frequent pain of childhood friendship in his drawing (Fig. 8.4b, p. 108). When someone is mean to him, he said, he deals with it by not playing with him. Although that is a good survival tactic, children also need to begin to develop conflict resolution skills and to find solutions with each other.

Ena Patricia's most difficult problem at the moment is her relationship with her son, Elvin. The aspect of their struggle she chose to focus on involved her teaching him the alphabet in Spanish (Fig. 8.5a, p. 109). She sees him as a resistant learner who becomes easily frustrated and has trouble focusing. When she punishes him by not allowing him to watch television, he becomes worried and applies himself to trying to learn.

Elvin's drawing touches on the same problem brought up by his mother (Fig. 8.5b, p. 110). The body pose and facial expression of the figure confirm his anger and discomfort. As he dictated his words and I wrote them down on the page, I asked him to explain why he "hated" doing his ABC's. He replied that they were too "long" and too "hard." I asked him how he thought he would learn best, and he told me with his "brain," but then he added that his mom and his aunt don't think he has a "good brain." I asked him to read what he had written for me. Because they were his words and had strong emotional content for him, he was able to reread them with few errors. I complimented him on how well he could read.

Ena Patricia and I looked at Elvin's words together. She wasn't surprised that Elvin had chosen to write about the same problem that she had for it is definitely a prominent struggle in their lives together. I suggested that perhaps teaching her son the ABC's as an isolated skill was not the best learning approach for Elvin who is such an active and mentally alert child. I suggested that perhaps he could dictate two sentences a day about something important to him and after she wrote down those sentences, he could add the illustrations. His words would become the text from which she would help him with the ABC's and other important skills. She listened carefully and seemed very pleased to hear my suggestion of another approach that might give her greater success and less pain.

Cynthia's children, Christina and Kris, wanted their "struggles" to be included in the book. Christina, the most academically advanced child in her first-grade classroom, said that her struggle lay in trying to write a story for her book (Fig. 8.6a, p. 111). In his illustration, Kris, her brother, was clearly thinking about the future: he wants to be a "famous basketball star" (Fig. 8.6b, p. 112). This is a popular aspiration for a ten-year-old boy, while at the same time reflecting a popular media image of the successful African American male.

Theme 4: Families as Protagonists of Their Own Stories

Design and Rationale

In the first book development session, I explained to the participants how to make a simple bound book with masking tape, needle and thread, and glue. At the end of the session, they had completed a book with blank pages, ready for words and illustrations. I then asked them

"Jessica and Her Friends" written by Henry Chamberlain, Directed by Jessica Chamberlain Taken from real life by Henry Chamberlain Edited on Tuesday, February 18, 1992 All Rights Reserved

Once upon a time there was a little girl named Jessica. This little girl lived in a little house in the woods. Whenever it wasn't raining she would go out into the woods to play with her friends the animals and to look at the rainbow.

But one day the little girl got sick and could no longer see the rainbow, cut flowers nor play with her friends the animals. Every night she prayed to God to make her well, so that she could return to play with her friends. The following day a little bird arrived at her window with a flower in his beak, he gave it to her and said, "We love you a lot Jessica and we want you to return and be with us again.

The little girl's love for nature and for the animals was so strong that when she saw how much all her friends loved her she quickly recuperated; and returned to the woods with all her friends.

All her friends were there waiting for her.. the rainbow and all her little animal friends. In honor of the little girl the rainbow displayed its brightest colors, and that is how Jessica lived very happily with all of them.

FIGURE 8.7a

to try to write a story in which their child and other family members appeared as the principal characters. I suggested that the parent could write the words and that the child could do the illustrations, or that the whole effort could be collaborative. I encouraged them to include photographs and collage materials (which as noted earlier were included in their supplies box).

Encouraging students and their families to write stories about themselves gives them the opportunity to become the main characters

FIGURE 8.7b

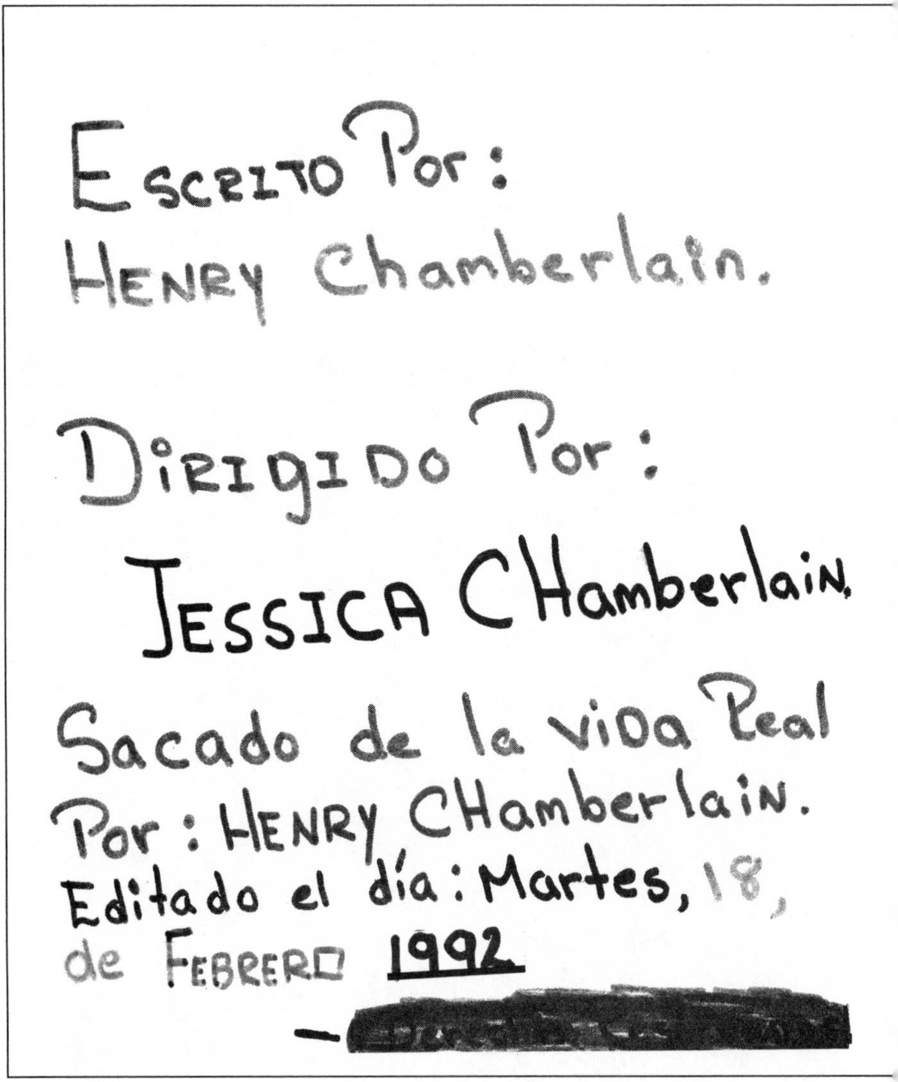

Escrito Por:
Henry Chamberlain.

Dirigido Por:
Jessica CHamberlain,

Sacado de la vida Real
Por: HENRY CHamberlain.
Editado el día: Martes, 18,
de Febrero 1992

FIGURE 8.8

JESSICA.
Y
SUS
AMIGOS.

Esta, niña vivia , en
CAda vez que dejaba de
a Jugar con sus amigos, los

FIGURE 8.9

una   casiTa   en el, Bosque.
llover , Ella   salia , al Bosque
animales y Contemplar el Arcoiris.

FIGURE 8.10

se enferno, y ya no
ar flores, ni jugar, con
Todas las noches, ella
bién, para volver a jugar
amigos.

Al dia Siguiente, llego
Ventana, con una flor,
y le dijo, nosotros te
queremos que vuelvas a

FIGURE 8.11

un   pajarito, hasta su
en su pico, se la entrego
queremos, mucho Jessica y
estar con nosotros nueva—
                    mente.

123

Allí, Todos sus amigos esp
y Todos, sus amiguitos los
niña, el arcoiris, dio sus
Jessica, vivio muy feli

FIGURE 8.12

e raban , por ella, el arcoiris,
animales. En honor a la
Colores, más fuertes y así
z con todos ellos.

of their own stories. As writers, they are able to create the characters, determine the events, and decide how they wish the story to end. The powerful experience of becoming an author is in strong contrast to their experience as ethnic or linguistic minority persons living in the United States and always being forced by the dominant culture to listen to and learn about someone else's story.

Analysis and Reflections

Henry and Jessica's Story.   Henry wrote a story about a little girl who lived in the woods and had a strong connection to nature (see Figs. 8.7–8.12, pp. 114–125). One day she fell sick and could no longer go out and play or enjoy her animal friends and the beauty of nature. Through the love of her friends, she was able to make a rapid recovery. The inspiration for this story was Henry's daughter, Jessica, who had suffered health problems during a period of several years. Henry said that he wanted to write a fantasy story about this aspect of their lives because in that way he could create the ultimate reality himself. At the second book development session, when Henry presented "Jessica y Sus Amigos," he described his experience as an author:

> Este pequeño librito nació del cerebro, mi modelo, porque la niña ha sido muy enferma y siempre hemos estado pendiente de su salud. Yo dije, "Voy a hacer un librito conforme a su enfermedad y voy a pensar . . . esta enfermedad no ha existido toda la vida porque algún día tiene ella que ver la cosa mejor, o sea ya sana. De allí pensé primero pongo que ella vive muy feliz, después se enferma vuelve a ser feliz otra vez. "Colorín colorado [este cuento se ha acabado]" porque ella queda ya sana y bien de salud.*

> [This little book was born from my brain, my model, because the little girl has been very sick and we have always been anxious and had to put many things on hold depending on how she was feeling. I said to myself, "I am going to make a little book about her illness and I am going to think . . . she has not been sick her whole life and one day she is going to see things better and be healthy. Then I thought, first I'll make her a little girl living happily, then she gets sick and then she goes back to being happy once again. "Colorín colorado" because she stays healthy and well].*

I have shared Henry's book several times with both teachers and parents, and everyone has been moved by its power—many, including myself, to tears. Creating the book was an act of love for Henry, not

---

*Henry is referring to the last page of "Jessica y Sus Amigos." "Colorín colorado" is the first part of a popular Spanish-language rhyming pattern; the second part here, "este cuento se ha acabado," means "this story is finished."

just for his daughter but for all of life. In his book, he explained: "¡Yo mezclé los dos sentidos, la tristeza con la alegría . . . la tristeza de la enfermedad y la alegría de ella por sobrevivir!" [I mixed the two feelings, sadness with happiness . . . the sadness of illness with the happiness of survival!] This book reveals the beauty and poetry inherent in a parent's words about something he knows and loves. Jessica and her classmates will easily learn to read the words from Henry's world. They themselves are the characters in the stories, and these stories can provide an engaging new text for emergent readers. Henry and Jessica together chose the photographs, stickers, and collage materials for their book.

Cynthia, Kristopher, and Christina's Story. This story (Figs. 8.13a–8.13b, pp. 128–129) was taped in Cynthia's apartment at the end of the second dialogue session. Cynthia had not yet begun to work on any of the book development projects and didn't know when she would find the time. She had also missed both group sessions, and so she did not have the benefit of the group dynamic that inspired the other participants. I worked with her and her two children separately one afternoon after school and told her I'd gladly help in any way she needed to feel successful in the process. I suggested that she discuss with her children what they would like the story to be about, and we could then record it. The only guideline was that they had to be the main characters. I would transcribe it to my computer, give them back their words, and then they could add the illustrations later. They all liked this idea.

Kristopher, the fourth-grade son, began a fantasy story, but Cynthia immediately stopped him. "I don't have an imagination, Kristopher, so it has to be something realistic." Kristopher wanted the story to be about talking cars and Christina about a park. After a few unsuccessful starts, the story began to take form, with Cynthia, the mother, providing the opening sentence.

The first theme to appear in their book was *education*. Because the family was trying to survive in the woods, education was of prime importance. *Independence* was the next theme. When the kids reached a certain age, about fifteen, it was time to leave the parents' home and make it in the world on their own. When they arrived in the city, the theme became *survival*. They tapped the knowledge they had acquired in the woods to make ends meet. They placed their values on independence and survival, and the results were running their own businesses and becoming the "owner."

Much like the characters in this story, Cynthia's own life is totally focused on a goal. Of course, as in the story, she recognizes that there will be "problems and step backs." First, she needs to complete the prerequisite nursing school courses; then she needs to attend nursing school,

FIGURE 8.13a

5

Chris went into his own furniture business since he likes the woods. He was the owner. The business started off slowly. He had to build and make the furniture first and find clients. As time went on, slowly but surely, eventually, he became a success. There were problems and step backs. It takes time.

6

Cat is this you
wht Play to eat
time? this
the Pog ca Name
All xchool go.

I taught them how to make paper dogs and I taught them how to write words.

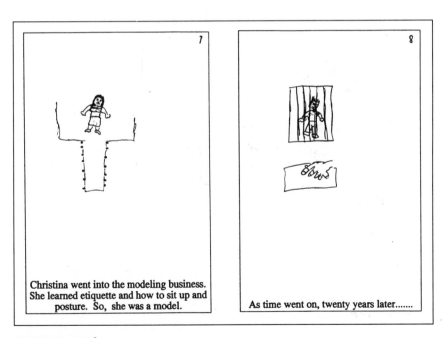

7

Christina went into the modeling business. She learned etiquette and how to sit up and posture. So, she was a model.

8

As time went on, twenty years later.......

FIGURE 8.13b

get a job, earn money, and move out of the housing project. In the meantime, she expects high academic performance from her own children, which they are achieving with ease. The point of the story is that people achieve success when they own their own businesses. As for modeling as a career, perhaps the media have persuaded her that being a successful model is an ideal.

Cynthia admitted that once she got started, her imagination could go along with her children's imagination. When I asked her what made her begin her story in a cottage in the woods, she laughed and said, "The first thing that popped into my head was Goldilocks." I told her how fascinating it was that in her attempt to write her own story, her strongest image was that of a blonde, curly haired little girl in a childhood story. These fairy tales are indeed universal, and the white European reality is unconsciously embedded in everyone's mind. This even holds true for Cynthia, an African American woman, a single mother who is living and struggling in a subsidized housing project, that is home to heavy drug users and with hardly enough trees to resemble the woods.

When Cynthia returned the transcribed story with her children's illustrations, I was surprised and disturbed by Kris's final illustration (see Figure 8.13b). "As time went on twenty years later . . ." depicted a person behind bars and a hand being finger-printed. Unfortunately, this drawing presents a potential reality for far too many African American males. Current statistics show that blacks make up 46 percent of all prisoners in the United States and are jailed at a rate four times higher than that in South Africa. More young U.S. black males are in jail, on probation, or on parole than in college. Nearly half of all black youth live in poverty, and about 60 percent live in households without a father (Karp, 1991).

Filmmaker John Singleton introduced his recent (1991) all-too-real portrayal of life in Los Angeles' African American community with the following statistical message: "One out of 21 Black American males will be murdered in their lifetime. Most will be killed at the hands of another Black male." Such images are constantly reinforced by the popular media. Kris is an excellent student and a wise perceptive child with fine ability to articulate the perils that surround him. Although I do not believe this illustration is Kris in twenty years, it certainly speaks to a child's concerns and uncertainties about his generation's future.

As for Cynthia, she is high-spirited and astute, and I believe she will get wherever it is she wants to go and will also find the best situations for her two children. No obstacle seems permanent or too tough for her to conquer.

Ena Patricia told how she and Elvin enjoyed looking through family pictures and writing about Elvin's life. Each page of their book contained a photograph and caption (Figs. 8.14a–8.14b, pp. 131–132).

*Estos fueron sus primeros
pasos en su cumpleaños en 1986.*

[These were his first steps on his birthday in 1986.]

FIGURE 8.14a

Siempre ha sido un niño alegre, entuciasta y muy energico en sus actividades.

[He has always been a happy and enthusiastic child and very energetic in all his activities.]

FIGURE 8.14b

Theme 5: Codification Based on Community Life

Design and Rationale

Through the dialogues, diverse themes emerged. I chose twenty words to concretize some of the major themes discussed and presented the words to Deborah Green, a San Francisco Bay area artist. Some of the words were *education, church, parks, technology, food, violence, just say no, pollution, nature, friendship, love, unemployment, television,* and *learning to read.* I asked Deborah to see if she could integrate the themes into a community scene through a line drawing. In her drawing, she effectively combined an outdoor and an indoor environment (Fig. 8.15, p. 134). Each participant and child was given a copy of the drawing and asked to develop a short story or narrative using the drawing as the point of reference and coloring or decorating the drawing as she or he wished. The intention was to give participants an in-depth opportunity to reflect on a visual representation of important aspects of their community reality.

Freire (1970) observes that the evolution of culture is marked by its passage through epochs, each of which is characterized by a series of "aspirations, concerns and values which man is searching to fulfill, as well as the obstacles to their fulfillment" (pp. 91–92). The themes of the epoch "in turn indicate the tasks to be carried out." These themes must be understood in order for change and transformation to take place. Freire believes that when these themes are not understood, then men and women become "dehumanized."

In this study, I chose words that appeared to have some importance in the lives of the participants as shown through the dialogues. Freire called these generative words. He often created "codifications" by setting generative words into simple, visual representations of the learner's reality. I decided to approach these themes in a similar manner.

Analysis and Reflections

In the story, or commentary, narrated by Nosisi (Narration 1, p. 135) with minimal assistance from her son, she speaks about what she actually sees and at the same time, she integrates her analysis of the situation. The violence, she says, stems from the people's frustrated efforts to find solutions to the problems they face in their lives. Despite this social tragedy, people can still find moments of joy that make life worth living. Children continue to play and adults continue to love.

Nosisi observes that the drawing is divided into two socioeconomic worlds, perhaps that of the "haves and the have nots." In the other

FIGURE 8.15

world, the one where she and Vuyo do not live, people still have their jobs, and so they have everything they need and want, including healthy pets. In her world, the anger that people feel is misdirected because they don't know on whom or what they should take out their frustration. They have not made the connections between their own situations and the broader societal problems.

NARRATION 1
Nosisi's and Vuyo's Story:
Codification Based on Community Life

Once upon a time there were no jobs. People were looking for jobs. There were some companies that were testing chemicals and the people were smoking these chemicals and getting cancer out of it. There were some people fighting. You can see that happen when you leave school and there are no jobs. The outcome is that people turn to drugs and they end up fighting on their own out of frustration while trying to find a solution.

Vuyo says that the people are eating pepperoni pizza.

What I see is that this picture is divided into two. In the upper part of the picture you can see all the frustration of drugs, jobs and everything, smoking the cancer and the chemicals. On the other side there are some kids jumping rope in the street and some positive things. There is a couple sitting and talking in the park which shows that whatever problems we have we can still make ourselves some enjoyment.

In the lower part of the picture, you can see a family behind the living room table full of fruits. Probably it's one of the families who at least still has a job. They have the table full of food and a pet that seems to be happy and they are eating pizza. One of the sons is doing a painting in the bedroom and one of the sons is watching the T.V. in the bedroom. The kids have toys. At least there is direction here. So, it's kind of a different picture from the one in the upper part. You can see in the bottom part it's a happy family together and they have everything. Everything is going well with them. They are far away from the top part of the picture where there is frustration, no jobs, drugs. Out of all that we can get some little bit of happiness. There's the couple talking on the side of the park while the kids are playing. It reflects what I see of life here. It's exactly where we are living. People are fighting in the picture because they see no solution. They don't know what to do and they don't know how to solve their personal problems and they also cannot direct their anger to what frustrates them.

In the hills people are taking a walk among the trees. They are happy catching fresh air.

Henry and his daughter, Jessica, first carefully colored Deborah's line drawing. Henry composed his words on a typewriter and gave them to me (Narration 2, p. 136). He divided his observations and feelings about what the line drawing said about the community into six categories, to which he referred to share his values and moral indignation. His statement begins by recognizing the need to educate the children. Vandalism, another category, is committed by people without education, he says. The churches provide the spiritual direction that people need to be at one not only with God, but also with other human beings. Henry demonstrates his awareness of ecological issues and the presence

NARRATION 2
Henry's Version of the Community Codification:
Nuestra Communidad

(1) EDUCACIÓN: Contamos con muchas escuelas para la educación y formación de nuestros jovenes. [EDUCATION: There are many schools for the education and formation of our youth.]

(2) IGLESIAS: Para la direccion cristiana y espiritual, que cada individuo necesita, para estar en bien con Dios y sus semejantes. [CHURCHES: For the Christian and spiritual direction that each individual needs in order to be at one with God and other human beings.]

(3) PARQUES: Punto clave para los niños y las familias, en donde hay relación con personas de diferentes, razas y costumbres, buen punto de relación. [PARKS: A key place for children and their families, where there is a meeting of people of different races and cultural backgrounds.]

(4) FÁBRICAS: Lugares de mayor destrucción del medio ambiente, tales como contaminación del aire, de los bosques, producto de muchas enfermedades, etc. [FACTORIES: Places of major destruction of the environment such as pollution of the air and forests, cause of many illnesses, etc.]

(5) VICIOS: Educar a nuestros hijos, dandoles información, sobre los peligros, que nos enfrentamos, día con día en las calles, de personas inescrupulosas, que ofrecen a nuestros hijos, caminos a la corrupción. [VICES: Educate our children by giving them information about the dangers which we come up against every day in the streets . . . unscrupulous people who lead our children down roads of corruption.]

(6) VANDALISMO: Tales como crimenes, asaltos, abuso infantil, corrupcion, etc. Todo esto se concentra entre personas sin educación, sin principios morales, y que nosotros podriamos evitar denunciando estos actos delictivos. [VANDALISM: Just like crimes, assaults, child abuse, corruption, etc. All this is concentrated in people without education, without moral principles, and we could avoid it by denouncing these delinquent acts.]

Hoy día existen muchos medios de comunicación, donde podemos obtener valiosa información, para la dirección, educación y formación, de nuestros seres queridos, que son nuestros hijos, los cuales se enfrentan, día a día, con mas peligros, y que nosotros como padres estamos en la obligación de mantenerlos alerta.

[Today there exist many means of communication from which we can acquire valuable information, for the direction, education and formation of our loved ones, our children. They are faced daily with more dangers and we as their parents have the obligation to keep them alert.]

of hazardous wastes when he speaks of the factories. His vision of the benefits of parks for families is very positive, for he embraces a multicultural appreciation of his community.

Both Henry and Nosisi recognize the themes of the "epoch" in their community. Many of the tasks to be carried out are implicit in their statements, and they have developed a critical attitude. Will they remain as onlookers, or will they begin to intervene in that reality? Could the home and the school together assume this kind of intervention into the problems of the community?

When Nosisi and Henry shared their versions of the narratives during the final group dialogue session, they were surprised at the different ways they each approached the subject. Henry appreciated how Nosisi integrated the ideas, whereas he in contrast had organized his interpretation into smaller thematic pieces. Their comments were most welcome, for this sharing, recognition, and appreciation of differences and similarities between participants from diverse communities was one of the goals of my study.

SUMMARY

In summary, the themes that were generated from the initial dialogues became the inspiration for the books that the participants and their families created. The words they wrote in their books enriched the study by providing additional insights into the participants' lives, histories, and aspirations. Despite the difficulties encountered in bringing these books to completion, all the participants were excited by the process and by the opportunity to engage in a literacy development project with their child. Ultimately, they were quite proud about what they had produced.

part 4

GENERATING NEW IDEAS: EMPOWERMENT THROUGH DIALOGUE AND THE CREATION OF BOOKS

chapter 9

Students, Families, and Communities Creating Knowledge

By the time students begin to reach the upper grades, they and their families have generally not been accustomed to an ongoing collaboration between the classroom, the home, and the community. Many, therefore, tend to show more resistance to the idea, since this kind of participation is unfamiliar to them. How can classroom teachers recognize and understand what such students in their classrooms know and feel? How can teachers help them to look critically at what they know, where they gained this knowledge, and how they can participate in acquiring and creating new knowledge and learning that they would see as useful and relevant in their lives? How can teachers help these students begin to explore family and community resources, using some of the same questions they are discussing in their classrooms?

In order to find ways in which teachers of older students may approach this work in their own classrooms and then branch out to families and the community, I began by inviting two fifth-grade boys who were classmates to dialogue with me. Hugo, a Latino student whose mother is Colombian, spoke both English and Spanish in his home, and Paul, a European American, spoke only English. I told them that through my work I had recently become aware that many teachers believe students don't really know very much, and I asked them what they thought about this assumption. Basically, they did not agree and were somewhat offended by the notion.

Hugo said that he thought a lot of his friends were really smart and good at figuring out things: "Paul is really good at artistic things like with his head and everything, like building things, and Samuel is smart at physical things like jumping fences and trees."

Paul thought that kids his age were adept at working out situations where "danger" was involved. Both agreed that school was their least favorite activity because it prevented them from doing what they really wanted to do. Their real interests were playing and exploring, which they considered the area in their lives where they could become the "smartest."

Because I was not a regular full-time classroom teacher at the time of this inquiry, I decided to discuss this issue with several friends who were. These teachers had valuable ideas for exploring the concept of students, families, and communities creating knowledge, and the following project developed from our discussions. This project was based on the belief that children have the ability to know and to create knowledge; they do not and cannot simply accept the knowledge that is handed down to them but must begin to discover abundance and richness in their own lives and communities. Students need to know who they are and that what they know matters. From here "they can find a place from which to stand and speak with dignity" (Giroux, 1990b).

AN EXAMPLE

I carried out this project in an Oakland, California, public school. The class was a fourth- through sixth-grade combination that was team taught by two teachers. In all there were sixty students; I worked with half the class for about two months. The students came from diverse racial, cultural and linguistic backgrounds reflecting the composition of the district. (I repeated this project two additional times, working with students from different classrooms who were of different age levels and language backgrounds.)

Getting Started

In a desire to be honest and clear with the students from the outset, I composed an introduction that I announced at our first meeting.

> I am a teacher working with other teachers to find out ways to help children to be the most that they can be and to learn the most they can learn.

I know that when children come to school, they already know a lot. If they are entering kindergarten, they have been learning for five years. The students in this classroom have been learning for ten, eleven and twelve years so you really know a lot. As babies and young children we learn a lot from our parents or from other adults who are caring for us. Our eyes are always open and we learn a lot about the world even before we begin to speak. In each home, children learn something different and important. No matter where you or your parents were born or what language you speak at home, teaching and learning are constantly taking place.

I would like to work with you for a few months to discover how many wonderful things you and your families all know and to see how we can share our knowledge with each other. It will be a kind of group investigation or research project. Through discussion and listening, all of us will participate in the making or creation of new knowledge.

There are no right or wrong ways to do this and there are no wrong answers. The thoughts and knowledge that each one of you has will be important. We will all contribute to this project by thinking and listening to each other, asking questions, doing interviews, being artists, writing and thinking all the time about how to do better what we are already doing. We will be creating new knowledge and turning this knowledge into personal books and also a group book. I would like to share with other teachers and students at the university the work you are doing during this project. I will then bring to you their reactions to your work and what they learned by reading your books.

The students were attentive, and no one asked questions for clarification. They were waiting to see where this would lead.

Using Music and Popular Culture as Texts

As a teacher, music and singing play an important part in my classroom work. Young students sing songs, internalize the words, and then use the written word as the reading text. Often they rewrite their own versions of the song. Song helps to bring any group of students together and move toward creating a classroom community. Singing lowers the anxiety level of the students and allows them to be receptive to the day's agenda. Because they are using more breath, more oxygen is flowing to the brain. Thus, they are thinking better.

To begin this particular project, I introduced a rap written by a good friend, musician and songwriter Kerrigan Black. The song perfectly integrates personal histories, learning, and the evolution of knowledge. Educators have Kerrigan to thank for this song, which he has carried around to many schools and recorded commercially and for which he has created a "teacher friendly" curriculum to build on the concepts presented in the song.

History Rap

Chorus:

You've got to know something 'bout history
So the world isn't just a mystery
You've got to know something 'bout history
So the world isn't just a mystery

For thousands of years, we've been making our way,
To get to where we are today,
Now, some folks don't think that's very far,
But they don't know how wrong they are.

Chorus:

History isn't just facts and dates,
It's different ways of living to appreciate,
It's what was happening long ago,
And what's going down in the times that we know.

Chorus:

History is me, and history is you
It's your mother, father, sister, brother,
grandparents too
It's the stars in the sky, the beat of the drum,
It's where you live, it's where you come from.

Chorus:

It's religions and rivers and mountains and kings
Fashions, inventions and crazy things!
It's art and music, war and peace,
Revolution, evolution that will never cease.

You've got to know something 'bout history so the world isn't just a mystery.

By Kerrigan Black/Heebie Jeebie Music. All Rights Reserved.

We were ready to begin, except that everyone was bouncing around in their seats, slapping their thighs and clapping, and they wanted to sing it again. Because I believe that there are many ways of responding to a text, and rhythm and rhyme is a powerful one, we sang it again. Although this kind of joyous response to music and words is typical for young students outside of the school environment, how often are they permitted this mode of interactive expression within a classroom setting? Teachers might think about bridging the gaps between school and nonschool learning by creating a space for popular culture as an arena for learning, analysis, and critique. Through their interpretation of the text, they will be creating new knowledge.

"What Does 'Knowledge' or 'Knowing' Mean to Me?"

Finally, I passed around slips of paper and requested that each student write one word, a few words, or a whole sentence, if desired, answering the question "What does 'knowledge' or 'knowing' mean to me?" After writing, they were asked to exchange their papers with another class member who would in turn read the statement to the entire class. I recorded on a large chart the words as they were spoken, including the student's name (in parentheses) for purposes of identification and ownership. The statements included the themes of education and its benefits, a human way of life, understanding meanings, and knowledge as the symbol of maturity and smartness. One student talked about "knowing things well and not forgetting." The session was lively, and students were interested in the definitions given by others.*

Students as Both Learners and Teachers

Next, the students were asked to think of a time in their lives when they taught something to a younger person. They were to write a description of the learner and the time and place of the teaching. They were also to reflect back on the learner's need to know and how they decided to teach that child. How did the child feel afterward, and how did they as the teacher feel?

This activity allows students to begin to view themselves in the dual role of both teachers and learners and to begin to experience and reflect on the learning act from both sides. It also enables students to remember that they indeed are teachers and will continue to be as they gain further knowledge. Recognizing the teacher capacity within each one of us also raises our self-esteem and allows us to be more receptive to new knowledge and to learning from others. It promotes a feeling of balance and wholeness.

Students were encouraged to illustrate their teaching experiences for their individual books; these illustrations were also to be included in the class collective work that would be part of the documentation for

---

*As students begin to explore their own opinions and knowledge, it is hoped that their understandings of who they are and how they have been formed by the sociopolitical context in which they live will help them to act critically in the larger community and society.

the project (see Figure 9.1). Although they were encouraged to use their primary language, none chose to do so.*

In the discussion that followed, the students identified four important themes: (1) a new sense of maturity gained when one becomes a teacher, (2) the urgency to help smaller people to survive, (3) the frustration often inherent in the act of being a teacher, and (4) the need to be persistent.

The following are the written responses of students to their role as teacher.

SPELLING

I taught my brother how to spell "box." He didn't know how to spell it so I showed him how. He needed to write a story. My brother was very happy. I was happy that he came to me instead of my mother and father.

FIGHTING

My niece is named Briona. She is four years old and I taught her how to fight in self-defense. It took her two weeks just to keep her fist balled up. First I taught her to hook a right. Second I taught her to upper cut a left. Then I let her practice on my stomach for a week. I taught her because this boy hit her at school. We both felt happy that she learned.

WRITING

I taught a five year old to write the letters A, B and C when I was nine. This kid was annoying. He didn't want to learn but his mother was afraid that since he was going into kindergarten and he didn't know how to write a little that he wouldn't get in. I tried for hours. First I guided his hand. That didn't work. Then I tried dot-to-dot making letters for him to connect. He connected wrong. I was really getting sick. The boy didn't even try. Finally he made a C. I was happy. I kept getting frustrated when he would not

---

*This particular classroom did not have a bilingual emphasis. English was the sole language of instruction. In addition, students at the grade 4–6 level are rarely still writing at school in their primary language unless they are recent immigrants and primary language instruction is still part of their daily learning.

In American education, the use of primary language is generally "transitional"—it is used only to help students to understand the content of the curriculum while they are acquiring English skills. The goal is not to maintain the first language or bilingual competencies but only to learn English. By failing to support the bilingual competencies of students who speak languages other than English, the American educational system is reducing the nation's multiple language capabilities. We remain basically a monolingual nation. It is ironic that at a later stage when students are interested in attending colleges or universities, they generally cannot be admitted without second-language capabilities. For students in this particular class, using their primary language at school no longer presented a possible or desirable option.

I taught a first grader named
Rachel how to read a book.
Afterwards she felt very happy.
I was happy too because I
accomplished something.
She was really excited about
reading because she just kept on
reading and reading. She likes
to go to the library and she
really is a very talented person. Erica

FIGURE 9.1

once I taught a smaller person ...
how to walk.

How to walk, He was 2 years old,

It was my brother, by holding,
his hand, they feel happy
I feel happay too

Meikan ___

FIGURE 9.2

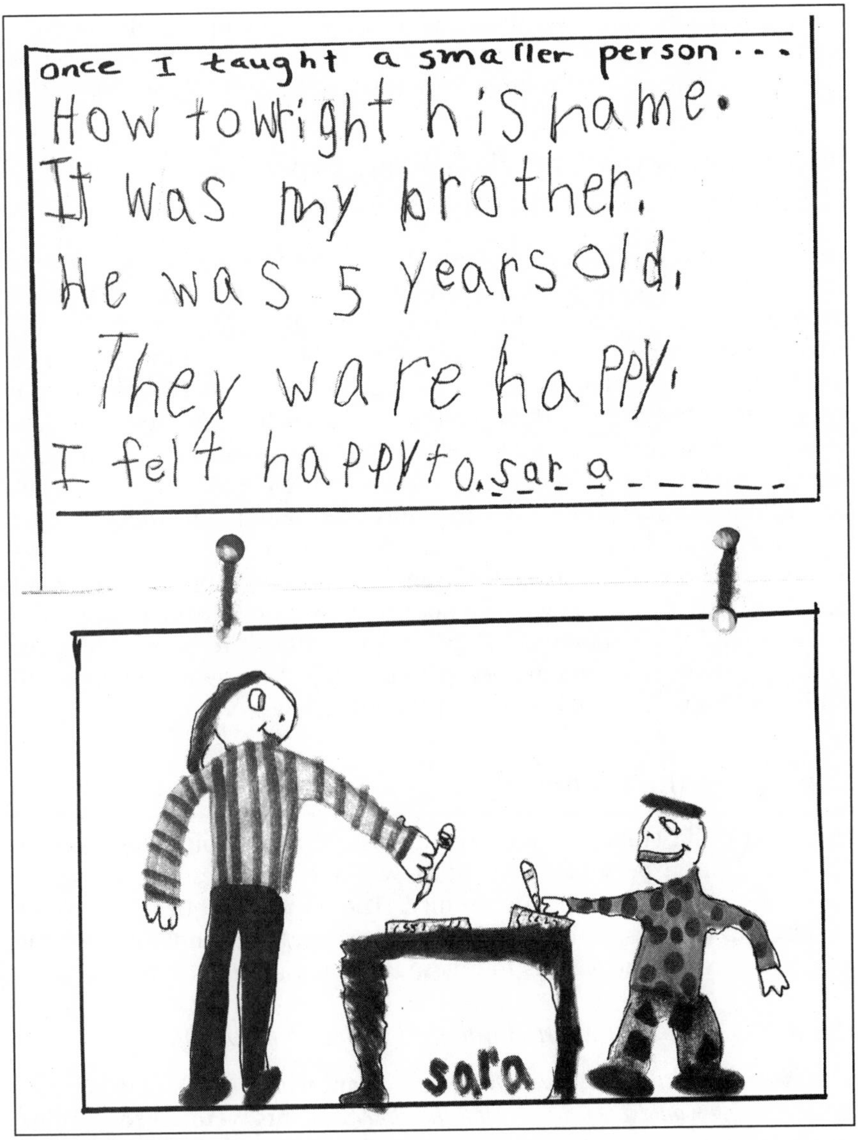
once I taught a smaller person . . .
How towright his name.
It was my brother.
He was 5 years old.
They ware happy.
I felt happy to. sara
sara

FIGURE 9.3

cooperate. Then came A. I did more hand guiding and dot-to-dot. Then B. I was tired, mad, and ready to throw up when he finally got it. He wasn't proud. All he wanted to do is go out and play. So did I.

I am also including writings and illustrations by first-grade children, who were involved in this project a few months later. Their work was carried out in a more structured format (Figs. 9.2 and 9.3, pp. 148–149).

Incorporating the Knowledge and Experience of Students' Family and Community

The next aspect of the project involved incorporating the knowledge and experiences of the student's family and community. Here the adults contribute to the creation of knowledge through dialogue with the students. In the project students were asked to bring home the very same questions that they had reflected on together in class. Through simple interviewing techniques, they were encouraged to write down or tape record the responses of family and community members. The students brought back and discussed the responses in the classroom. What similar or different definitions did the adults offer about "knowledge?" The students explored factors such as age and cultural and generational differences. "Knowledge means to know what is good for you and what isn't." "Knowledge is a key to the door of education." "Knowledge is experience and understanding." How are our parents' responses different from our own? The students began to develop their own wall charts to study the information gleaned from the interviews.

Expanding the Dialogue

Each week the students explored, discussed, and wrote about a new question from a personal point of view. Then the question was taken back to the family and community. The kinds of questions to be explored in relation to the theme of "knowledge" are numerous. As one question is posed, new areas to investigate emerge.

Building Bridges between Home and School Knowledge

What do I really know well that is important *to me? How and where did I learn it? How would I teach it to someone else?* Students were asked to think about and focus on realms of knowledge that are not acquired as part of their school learning process. In this way, teachers can begin to reach out and validate alternative forms of learning by the student, family, and community and students can begin to understand that learning and the acquisition of knowledge is a lifelong process that does not begin and end at the schoolhouse door. Multiple forms of learning and knowledge acquired can be shared in the classroom to enrich the lives of all the students. Knowledge gained can be brought back and shared in the community or even exchanged between other classes within the same school. This part of the project raised such questions as: How does the knowledge that students have already gained from home relate to what the school wants them or expects them to know? How do the students themselves view the connection between the two?

READING

I think that I am very good at reading. I think that reading is a very special thing to accomplish. . . . It takes me to far away places. I learned to read with my mother. She used to read to me at night and soon I learned to memorize the words. I have always been in a higher reading level than my grade. If I were to teach someone, I would probably start out with them sounding out with the words.

SPEECHES

What I know well is speeches. The man I learned from was Dr. Martin Luther King Junior. I learned that the art of speeches is expressing yourself in a civilized way. If I could, I would teach people about making speeches.

A second grader spoke about his skill in maze construction (Fig. 9.4, p. 152).

Many students connect their out-of-school learning experiences with a special or respected adult whom they see as a model of desirable knowledge or skills that they are eager to imitate or participate in.

This same question ("What do I really know well that is important to me?"), when posed to parents, especially those with limited years of formal schooling, can be threatening and empowering at the same time. The adult questions the validity or appropriateness of her response. "Is this what the teacher wants to hear? Is this real knowledge or just something I've learned in order to survive? Will my own child be ashamed of me?" Students may be asked to theorize about what forms of knowledge they believe their parents possess. What do they think are their parents' skills and wisdom? Do they think that their parents would agree with their evaluation? How will they reconcile their own beliefs to their parents' reality?

One positive result of interactions between classroom and home is that teachers can really begin to communicate interest and caring toward all students that enter the classroom. All responses are worthwhile because they are an expression of the humanity and history of each family. Families become more willing to share their experiences and thoughts as they come to believe that the teacher is sincere, that their own child values the information given, and that they themselves can in fact contribute to the education of their children. Parents, as well

FIGURE 9.4

as students, are encouraged to respond in their first language. Students can serve as translators to those who may not understand. Multilinguality is always to be encouraged and supported as we rethink the educational process. Ada and Beutel (1991) point out the value of transcribing the words from a participatory dialogue. Transforming the dialogues into a printed text imbues them with a new prestige. The texts become "music" to the ears of those who have never seen their own words in print.

One mother, a recent immigrant from Mexico, works in a cannery. Although she is glad to be in this country and to be able to provide her children with what she believes to be a high-quality educational experience, she feels that she has had to learn to act like a machine and not complain.

> Aunque estoy feliz de tener un trabajo con lo cual yo puedo mantener a mis hijos, a veces yo siento como si fuera yo la máquina. Estoy aprendiendo de aceptar mi aburro sin quejar.
>
> [Although I am glad to have a job with which I can support my children, sometimes I feel like a machine. I am learning to be bored without complaining.]

Several parents wrote about skills they had acquired from family members.

> I know how to cut hair well. When I was young I would watch my brother do my friend's hair. When I got older, I decided that was something that I wanted to do. My father sent me to barber school, and I learned how to cut hair good.
>
> I know how to bake real well. I learned at an early age in my mom's kitchen. My mom taught me how to bake. I had lots of practice and practice makes perfect, or makes you good at whatever you do. [Fig. 9.5, p. 154.]

One father spoke about his natural evolution into architecture and how it has entered into every aspect of his life (Figure 9.5).

Using Life Experience Knowledge for Problem Solving

Solving problems is one way in which people use knowledge gained through life experiences to move forward and to improve their lives. In the next stage of the project, students were asked to *talk about a difficult problem they have had to face in their lives and how they used their own knowledge to solve it.* In general, the young students seemed to see their problems in the immediacy of the present. They wanted to get themselves out of difficult situations and return to spaces of comfort and acceptance. Many of their problems focused on interpersonal peer issues of acceptance and rejection. They spend a great deal of time thinking about who

I Know how to bake really well. I learned at an early age in my moms Kitchen. My mom taught me how to bake. I had lots of practice and practice makes perfect or makes you good at what ever you do.

I know architecture really well, but the nice thing about it is that you are constantly learning. I learnt it from my own father. When I was a growing child, I loved to draw so, regularly, I spent hours at my dad's office in Beirut drawing and watching him draw. Thus, naturally I became an architect. Also we used to discuss architecture at dinner time. As a matter of fact, I married an architect. So you see how much architecture is a part of my life. I studied it for seven long years in Beirut and Oxford and now I practice it here.

FIGURE 9.5

they are, how they should act to win or maintain friends, and how to eliminate what causes them pain or frustration.

ACCEPTANCE

My problem was that in the fourth grade everybody thought that I couldn't play sports and they wouldn't let me play. I tried to show them I was good. One day they let me play and they were proud. From that day on they let me play every day.

PRIVACY

My problem is that my brother is always messing with my stuff and messing up my room. Now I put a lock on my door.

GETTING WHAT YOU WANT

I had a problem where I had to lie in order to be able to go outside and play. But instead, I used my knowledge and realized that I should not lie. So, I told the truth and I got to go outside and play.

BAD HABIT

My problem was a habit. I sometimes stuttered and made high pitched sounds. I didn't think I could stop. One day my mother told me to stop and I couldn't. Then my mother threatened me with her thick leather belt. And I stopped right on the spot.

SCHOOL

My problem is school. I hate it. It stinks man. Torture! *Help!* How to get it solved? Well, just drop out.

As teachers, we need to listen to and accept the idea that what our students tell us represents a problem for them. A deeper truth often lies behind what may appear to be a superficial verbal utterance. At first, students may feel uncomfortable exploring hidden feelings. From my own childhood I remember the expression, "Many a true word is said in jest." Their short statements bear the seeds for much further discussion, analysis, and writing on topics such as fairness and equity, respect for private property, reasons young people feel inadequate, questions of truth, reasons for holding onto bad habits, corporal punishment and child abuse, and negative feelings about school. Students first need to know that their words have been heard, and then they have the opportunity to understand more fully the causes of their feelings. This can be followed by brainstorming, both individually and within the group, about how issues can be confronted, and how the "what is" can become the "what they wish to be." In this way, each student can be a winner in his own life journey.

Empowerment through Valuing Alternative Forms of Knowing

Throughout the project, students were encouraged to explore alternative forms of knowing. They began to understand that the dominant group in the society, through schooling, traditionally dictates what knowledge is important and what knowledge is worth being taught and learned. When students are not part of the dominant culture or do not speak the dominant language fluently, they begin to realize that their knowledge, as well as that of their family and community, is of lower status. This project is empowering in that it involves the students in the exploration, interpretation, and creation of knowledge and allows them to discover and validate the importance of their own knowledge. They come to feel wiser, smarter, and thus more powerful. They also begin to realize that when people hold power in their schools, district, or country, this also legitimates their particular forms of knowledge which they can then impose on others.

The next phase of the project elicited the student's definition of "power." *What does power mean to you?* Some of the responses from the group of fourth- to sixth-grade students were money, ruling, brave, conquer, adrenalin, muscles, God, horsepower, publicity, wind energy, control over yourself, good looks, controlling other people, and knowing how to play video games.

They were then asked to think about *what they'd like to know or learn most and how they thought they might acquire this knowledge. Would that knowledge give them* power? *How would they use the power they gained?*

TO STOP WARS

I would like to know how to stop wars. I think I could get this knowledge by years and years of studying. It would be hard but worth it because then anybody's friend wouldn't have to get killed. It would give me power because everybody would like to be smart like me.

TO RUN A BUSINESS

I would like to be able to run a business to make more money and to help people get a job by having employees to work for me.

TO BE A LAWYER

What I like to learn is law. I think law is important because this world is not equal so that's why when I grow up I want to be a lawyer. People always deserve the best in everything.

TO READ MINDS

I would like to read minds. To read minds is also being psychic in a different way. If you can read minds then you can hear ghosts because ghosts are the minds of dead people. With this power I will help to solve murders and I could also learn how to get knowledge from people who have more power than me. If this would happen, it would be a dream come true.

Young students not only have fantastic imaginations, but they are also not afraid to talk about reaching for the impossible. In their yearning for new knowledge and power, they demonstrate clearly that they are children who have grown up in a world consumed by the fear of war and violence. They know well the realities of unemployment and joblessness, and they want to help their fellow human beings in their striving toward justice and fair treatment. Several of their statements reveal a clear acceptance of and fascination with the world of death and the supernatural.

Confronting Obstacles to Acquiring and Creating New Knowledge

Finally, we delved into the meaning of two sophisticated words: *"obstacle"* and *"confrontation." What obstacles do you think could stand in the way of learning and knowing what you want to know, and how will you confront them?* Some of the words evoked for "obstacle" were challenge, writer's block, injury, conspiracy, dumb teachers, and poor guidance. For "confrontation" they suggested persuade, standing up to, try harder, presentation of your idea, use knowledge, and conversation.

RUN A SMALL BUSINESS

I would like to run a small business. The obstacles are getting the business started. I would have a gospel music store. I would find the place and then get a loan. I would find where to get my music. Then I would find an employee.

POOR GUIDANCE

The obstacles that can get in my way of becoming a lawyer is bad teaching or poor guidance. The way I would confront this would be to get the information from others.

RACISM

If I am going to be a doctor, what I think could get in my way is racism. I would be the best that I could be and a lot of people would be upset because I made it and they didn't. There might not be a lot of racism but there is enough to start segregation in this world.

Students were aware not only of the reality of economic conditions and the presence of racism in their world but also of ways human beings compete and fight with each other. They recognize when others do not want them to get ahead or when poor-quality education is holding back their own possibilities for success. The young girl who refuses to use poor education as an excuse for her own failure is committed to transforming her own life. Teachers need to help students explore the immediate obstacles they encounter in acquiring new knowledge as well as to move beyond personal blame and purely personal solutions. Students will begin to discover that the problems and obstacles they uncover are endemic to our society and sometimes are even universal.

INITIATING THE PROCESS OF CREATING NEW KNOWLEDGE

The project discussed in this chapter carries multiple possibilities for expansion throughout the school year. However, it will still be important to continue to be true to the four basic assumptions that form the foundation for this work.

- Teachers and their students together are co-participants in the learning process.
- New knowledge is built on old knowledge.
- Parents and communities need to be seen as equal contributors of understanding and knowledge to the educative process.
- All people are capable, through analysis and critique, of engaging in actions that may transform their present realities.

chapter 10

Additional Themes for Student, Family, and Community Books

By now you will have gained a real sense of the importance of student voice in the classroom, the contribution of the voices of family and community, and the realities of building a curriculum with these voices as a central focus. In this chapter, I outline in detail additional suggestions for developing book themes that will extend the concepts presented earlier. Teachers should feel completely comfortable about interpreting and carrying out the ideas in any way that is appropriate to their particular classroom experience. All the suggestions that follow should be seen within the context of a transformative pedagogy in which the teacher is seeking a collaboration between classroom, student, family, and community.

Because one of the teacher's most valuable tasks is to nurture the relationship between the students and their families, it is necessary to communicate that parental knowledge is important both to their children and to the teacher. Through their position of respect, teachers can offer parents an opportunity to speak about their life experiences and, by giving this knowledge an important place in the classroom, help the students better appreciate their parents.

POINTS TO CONSIDER

The following considerations may be relevant to the development of co-authored or collaboratively written books.

1. Choose a selection of literature, poetry, or a song to introduce the new theme.
2. Begin with a brainstorming session about the theme being initiated and perhaps relate it to the literature selection. All students should be encouraged to participate orally and to relate their own experiences about the subject. This may be carried out with the whole class, after which students may break into small groups for further discussion and work.
3. Record any important new vocabulary being used and the thoughts of the students to further validate their contributions.
4. If an interview format has been chosen for the book, have the students formulate the questions to be asked to the participants. The format may consist of a single question to be asked orally, or can be a written questionnaire with space for responses. For older students, the use of a tape recorder may be explored. This would allow students to transcribe or listen to the responses several times and then extract what they hear as the most important themes.
5. Discuss, map, or thematically organize information brought to the classroom on wall charts. This will allow visual learners to also experience the richness of the responses and all students to interact with print.
6. Make many of the books joint efforts between the students, their families, and communities, although often the student will have the task of weaving the stories and the multiple points of view together into a single book. Other books can be written at home in co-authorship and arrive at school in their finished form.
7. Have some books begin with the student's own first draft of the text. This first draft should provide the student with an unrestricted opportunity to put down ideas creatively. This is not the time to focus on the details of conventional writing. Students may edit each other's work before the final book is ready for "publication."
8. Choose some form of bookbinding. It can be a simple blank-paged book that the teacher has stapled together, or it can be more elaborate with a sewn binding, fabric cover, and intricate illustrations.
9. Create a ritual for celebrating the authors and the completed books in order to inspire students and their families to continue the process. Students from other classrooms may be invited

during the day, or the event can be held in the evening so that families may participate and read their own works.

ADAPTING, EXTENDING, AND CREATING THEMES

I have chosen to begin the practical application of this book with an activity that is broad in scope. It shows how the range of possibilities can be expanded for any of the following activities. As we explore other examples, I trust that your understanding of the process will allow you to determine the level of complexity of the project you choose. Your familiarity with your students and their age-specific abilities, as well as your own experiences, will eventually determine the focus and range of questions. Most of these activities can be programmed into two days or expanded into a project encompassing a period as long as two weeks, a month, or the entire year.

The first activity is of central importance to every aspect of the philosophy presented in this book. It is hoped that this activity will be initiated early in the year. It provides parent/child interaction, it places students in their history, and it builds self-esteem. In addition, it provides basic information about your students and their families. The process of sharing this information allows students to discover their similarities and differences and facilitates a process of bonding within the classroom community. It also provides you, the teacher, with information that can form the basis for the other activities during the year. Ultimately, it presents information that is vital to understanding the depth of experience that your students and their families bring to your classroom. This knowledge can be used to build and expand your curriculum for the entire year.

THEMES

Our Family History

Objective

This activity is designed to facilitate an interaction between the students and their parents as they explore their roots and the community in which they live. The students will come to a better understanding of their place in the history of the family and in their world. Through sharing and putting together a group book, students in the classroom will come to know and appreciate the similarities and differences in their histories. This information will provide opportunities for further discussion and activities across the curriculum.

Process

1. Students and teacher develop a list of questions to ask their parents, including:
   - Where were your grandparents born, and where did they grow up? What school experiences did they have, and what kind of work did they do? Are they still living? With whom do they live? What language do they speak at home?
   - Where were your parents born, and where did they grow up?
   - Where were you born, and where did you grow up?
   - What is your happiest childhood memory, and will you illustrate it for our class book?
   - If you are now living in a different country or community than before, what do you like most and least about your new home, and what do you miss most or least about your old home?
   - What kind of work do you do now? Are you satisfied doing this work, or would you prefer to do something different?
   - What are your dreams for your children?
2. As the students bring back their responses, the teacher reads them out loud with great interest and praise for the parents' contribution. Other students, looking forward to similar teacher and class responses, will be motivated to bring their part to school more quickly.
3. The words and drawings can be put together in a book with a title such as "Our Family History."
4. The teacher, using large chart paper, can help the children to analyze and record the parent responses into commonly occurring themes and categories.
5. The book can be placed in the classroom or school library or used as a personal tool for building reading skills.
6. A photocopied summary of parent responses can be sent home with each child so that parents can begin to know about each other. It is hoped that they will begin to build a community to support not only their children but also each other.
7. Children may take turns bringing home the class book, protected in a large zip-lock bag, to read at home with their families.

Suggestions and Reflections

This particular book holds many possibilities, and you may choose to focus on any aspect of family history. You will notice that several other books suggested here are extensions of this theme. This book was recently used in a third-grade classroom with a group of children whose parents had immigrated from Mexico. A map of Mexico was constructed, and the children discovered that all the parents came from four different states. They realized that most of their parents' happiest moments were those associated with times of traditional festivities. They also discovered that the majority of their parents were very happy to be living in the United States, although they had fears and concerns for the future of their children.

Teachings from My Childhood Community

Objective

The development of this book will give parents an opportunity to talk about memories of the place where they spent their childhood. For some, these memories will be quite vivid, while for others who may have experienced many changes and geographical moves, memories may be more nebulous and even painful.

Every community, no matter how small, has its customs and traditions that children learn about quite early in their lives. The climate, the landscape, or the kind of work done by the people will influence the knowledge passed on. Sometimes resurrecting these memories reclaims lost knowledge.

The creation of this book, which elicits parent memories, also gives students an opportunity to think about the town or city in which they are living and going to school. What knowledge do they gain on a daily basis by simply living there?

Process

1. Think about our own community. Where do people get their food? Do they know where to go when they want to have fun? What are the dangers that exist in the community, and how do young people learn to protect themselves from these dangers? Does the area have neighborhoods that are distinct from one another in any way? Is the town multiethnic and multilingual, or is the population homogeneous? Why? What is the history?
2. Have each student choose to discuss, write about, or illustrate one piece of knowledge they have gained from living in their community. These individual contributions may be turned into a group book, "What We Know about Our Community."
3. Ask parents to share their memories with their children either orally or in writing.

Suggestions and Reflections

For immigrant students knowledge from their homeland is essential. One of my students shared knowledge he had gained in his village

Mi Papá me dijo que no
cominara debajo de los árboles
de Papaya porque alli viven
los alacranes y ellas pueden
caer en mi cabeza.

FIGURE 10.1

164

in Jalisco, Mexico. In this village, he told the class there were many papaya trees, and everyone loved to pick and eat the fruit. Village children were warned not to play under the trees because the *alacranes* (scorpions) like to sleep there. They could jump down onto your head and bite you hard (see Figure 10.1).

The Wise One

Objective

Webster's dictionary defines "wisdom" as a "store of knowledge." We all know people in our lives whom we would consider wise, even though their formal school education was perhaps brief. Through the creation of this book, it is hoped that students will recognize or get to know a person who possesses "wisdom" and that parents will also take time to think about someone they have known who possessed a nontraditional form of knowledge. It can be a way of honoring and validating alternative knowledge gained through living and reflection.

Process

1. Brainstorm with the students the meaning of the word "wisdom." Look up definitions in several different dictionaries and compare them with the definitions supplied by the students.
2. Read folk tales in which an important character is a wise person. Why is this character considered wise by the people in the village? Where do her or his powers lie? (with humans, animals, plants, or the forces of nature?)
3. Ask the students to talk about people in their lives that they consider to be "wise."
4. Assign a short descriptive sketch of the "wise one" in their lives accompanied by a drawing to capture his or her essence (Fig. 10.2a–10.2b, pp. 166–167; Fig. 10.3a–10.3b, pp. 168–169).
5. Have the students ask their families or someone in the community the following: "Think of a person you have known in your life, either in childhood or later, who possessed some special knowledge or powers and was respected and admired by the community." It should preferably be a person who has had little or no traditional schooling. Why were these persons special, and what did they know or could they do?
6. As the character sketches are returned to school, ask that they be read, and as students react to the wisdom portrayed, discuss similarities and differences in the types of wisdom shared.
7. Invite to the classroom a community person who has been identified as a "wise one." Students may prepare questions in advance to guide them in an interview. Take photographs of the

Mi Abuelita "Lola" Fue una persona muy sabia para mi. Por que me enseño a ser muy responsable y Trabajadora. Tambien Tenia mucho conocimionto en yarbas, flores. y Tambien preparaba muchas comidas ricas y deliciosas. — la extraño mucho.

FIGURE 10.2a

FIGURE 10.2b

FIGURE 10.3a

HELLO MY NAME IS DENISE FRIAS VANESSA
MOTHER. I HAVE A GREAT MEMORY OF A MAN. HE
CAME FROM BRAZIL. HAD NINE KIDS HE WORKED
AT THE PERISIAN BAKERY MOST HIS LIFE AND HE
WORKED VERY HARD. HE WAS ALSO VERY WISE MAN
HE INVENTED A NEWSPAPER MACHINE, EGGCRACKER,
AND A ROCKING CHAIR. YOU WOULD HAVE TO SEE IT.
TO BELIEVE IT. THIS MAN PAST AWAY AND WENT TO
TO HEAVEN. NOVEMBER 25. 1992. HIS NAME WAS
            JOSE DE SILVA FRIAS

MY FATHER, VANESSA GRANDFATHER, A GREAT.
MEMORY AND A WISE MAN. HE WAS.

FIGURE 10.3b

students with the visitor. The following day, students can write about the experience and their impressions. This may also be a group account, with the text developed in a round-robin fashion.

Suggestions and Reflections

This project provides opportunities for spontaneous field trips and walks in the community. Visits with "wise" persons in their home or workplace can be arranged to allow students to conduct interviews. New knowledge of the community will engender a deeper feeling of respect for its inhabitants.

One first-grade California teacher chose to integrate the exploration of wisdom to coincide with International Women's Day. The class was an ethnically and economically diverse group of students whose levels of developing literacy spanned a wide range. Students were asked to write about a time when they were wise, and parents were asked to write about a wise person in their own lives who influenced them. The students also studied the lives of many women who have made important contributions to humanity.

Because of the student's desire also to acknowledge the women at their school, the project was extended to include video interviews with faculty and staff at the school. The project culminated with a multimedia school assembly presentation of the work produced by the students, the mothers, and the women staff at the school. The classroom teacher summed up the experience as follows:

> Students were extremely enthusiastic because they were recognized for their own wisdom and became aware that wisdom was to be found at their school, in the community, in their homes and within themselves. They had the opportunity to share the stage with all the important grown-up women from principal, to cafeteria workers to secretary who they honored with bouquets of flowers. (Spatz, 1993) (Fig. 10.4, p. 171; Fig. 10.5, p. 172.)

Parent's Dictionary

Objective

By constructing this book, the students will acquire an appreciation of the richness and beauty of human language. Everyone has words that are special to them. In her book, *Teacher* (1969), Sylvia Ashton-Warner describes a key word approach for teaching initial reading. Key words carry strong associative meaning for children, generally relating to important experiences in their lives and proving to be the words that the children will learn to read quite easily. They are words that radiate from their own natural vocabulary, and often they are words that have just been learned and that the child finds very exciting, provocative, or useful.

my MOM IS wISe beCause she Khows more than all the peaple In my House.

Jacob   Jewett

FIGURE 10.4

My MOM is wise because she can take care of two children at a time and still have an important job working wid computers

FIGURE 10.5

Young children enjoy playing with words. As teachers, we can encourage this enthusiasm and facilitate the growth of vocabulary in many ways. Asking the parents to send in words that represent something important in their lives not only can build on the students' vocabularies but also can give them insight into their parents' lives.

Process

1. Have the students develop a "wall dictionary" in the classroom. First the names of the students are placed in alphabetical order. A math activity may follow in which the students graph and tally how many names fall under the same letter. New words are added each day through literature and discussion. The dictionary is large, highly visible, and a great resource that students will refer to frequently during writing activities. The words will be remembered and used because they are their own.
2. Ask the students to collect new words from adults in their home. They must also know the meaning of each word they bring.
3. In their small groups, have the students share the words from home. Each can teach the others a new word that belongs to his or her family. Students can be encouraged to use words from their home language.
4. Compile the combined words of the students and their parents into a simple dictionary book that can be easily reproduced and sent home with each student.

Suggestions and Reflections

Researching words is a wonderful introduction to the world of research for students. They can ask many people they know, "Tell me your three favorite or most important words"— a question that not too many people would be reluctant to answer. As a result, vocabulary and command of language will increase rapidly.

My Mother or Father Is Special

Objective

The primary purpose of this book is to honor and validate the student's parents—their lives and abilities, their ideas and aspirations. The book may also focus on another important adult in the child's life. When the teacher and the school demonstrate real interest and respect for the student's parent, this promotes higher self-esteem for the student. When the students feel that their homes and parents are accepted, they not only accept themselves more fully but are also better able to feel motivated and successful at school. It is also important for a student to hear about the problems that their parents may have experienced in life and of their attempts to resolve them. This allows them to see that working hard or struggling to make a better life is a worthwhile endeavor.

Process

1. Lead a discussion with the students about their mothers and fathers. Discuss what they think it means to be a mother or father. What do they think their parents do all day? Do they think being a parent is difficult? Where do they think their mother or father learned how to care for a child? Do they think their parents are satisfied with their lives? Do they believe that their parents would like to change anything about their lives?

2. Help the children design a questionnaire that will provide the information needed to make a book about these special persons, their mother or father. When you send the questionnaire home, you may also invite the parents to send photographs of themselves as children and pictures of themselves with their own children.

3. Upon return of the questionnaire, ask the students to decide how they would like to use the information to design their books. The students may choose to use all the parents' own words, or they may use pieces of the responses and augment these while creating their own story about the parent.

4. Have each student decide individually how many pages his or her book will have, how many thoughts will go on one page, and where he or she will place illustrations and photographs.

5. Encourage the students to take turns reading finished books to the rest of the class.

6. Send this particular book home as a gift, perhaps for Mother's Day or Father's Day or as a birthday present.

Suggestions and Reflections

When I began to do this project with the students, I started by making a book about my own mother. I spent the good part of a weekend going through my family albums and talking to my mother on the telephone. I wanted to share something of my own life with my students and to communicate the love and support I felt from my mother. I focused on aspects of my own emerging literacy and on how much I loved it that my mother read me stories. The students requested that the book be read several times. I felt that it was a good way to initiate this project, and my own enthusiasm helped theirs to take root.

I would encourage teachers to share more of their personal life experiences with their students. Sometimes we think that this is "unprofessional" or that the mandates of our curriculum do not leave time for this kind of sharing. In reality, however, it sends students the message that their teacher would also like to know about their lives. It gives them the freedom to use their voices.

Words of Advice from Our Parents

Objective

The transmission of values has been at the core of every civilization. Students need to know what their elders consider important and what expectations their elders have for them. What words of wisdom do parents feel obligated to pass on? What words does each new generation receive from its family or cultural group through advice, ritual, and tradition?

Process

1. Send home a short letter to the parents which may read something like this: "Pretend for a moment that you are going on a long journey and are not sure when or if you will return. What advice would you give to your children before departing?"
2. As the students bring back their responses (written, taped, or orally shared) hold small group discussions about how they feel about their parents' words and whether they were aware of these values before the parent shared them. In what way does the student feel that his or her parent had already communicated those values?
3. Look for the similarities in responses about what parents want for their children. Do the students feel they will be able to live up to their parents' expectations?

Suggestions and Reflections

The question about last words of advice will be highly emotional for some families and only matter of fact for others. Last year, one parent confided in me that she cried while writing her responses but that she felt it had been important for her to be able to think about and take the time to put down her thoughts in written form.

The development of this book can offer parents the opportunity to think deeply about their role as parents, to focus on the nurturing and loving aspects of their relationship with their children, and perhaps even to save a little more quality time each day to share themselves with their children. The presence of this book in your classroom library reminds students each day of who they are, how much they are loved, and the resources they bring to school.

Friendship across Generations

Objective

The theme of friendship is discussed throughout the school years. This subject includes the extreme moments of joy and grief in the student's life, and much of the best literature for young readers revolves around this theme. This book is developed so that each member of the family can discuss what friendship means to them. It allows students and parents to discuss the special qualities of their friendships and commitments to others. It recognizes that human relationships may go through difficult periods but that we are capable of finding ways to resolve our differences and work through our problems. While contributing to the book, parents are given the opportunity to look into their past and to share their memories with their children. The process gives the student a glimpse of the child within his parent. This sharing can help parents to be more sensitive to and understanding of their children. (The subject of friendship was presented earlier in the book, Chapter 8, in the extended research project with first-grade families.)

Process

1. Brainstorm with your students or invite them to discuss in small cooperative groups what friendship means to them. How can we be a good friend to someone?
2. Ask each student to think about a special friend and to write about or draw a portrait of that friend.
3. Have the students conduct interviews with each other and later interview their parents.
4. Have the students use the following guiding questions in their interviews of each other or of an adult in the family about a friend from their childhood or youth.
   - What was special to you about your friend?
   - Why do you think you were special to your friend?
   - What were the similarities and differences between you and your friend?
   - What did you enjoy most doing together?
   - What could you have done for your friend or she for you that would have made you both happy?
   - Did you ever have a problem or disagreement with your friend, and how did you resolve it?
   - Do you think friendship could help solve the world's problems? Why?
5. Assign several different books in this project. Students can make books about each other; they can make books about their par-

ents' friends; or they can combine their own thoughts about friendship with the contributions of family members and they will be on the way to producing a book that can be cherished for years to come.

Suggestions and Reflections

In working with students, it is usually more meaningful to begin with the personal before reaching beyond. The discussions, activities, and writing on friendship can lead to an exploration of relationships in the children's community, nation, and world. What is the power of friendship? What obstacles do we face in developing friendships with people we perceive to be different from ourselves? What can we do to confront these obstacles? What does the phrase "hands across the world" mean? Is language a barrier to friendship? How could the world be a better place for all people if individuals and groups were committed to developing friendships?

As a class activity, you can seek out a group of children in another school or a foreign country for correspondence—"pen pals." In addition, some organizations facilitate international communication through computer relationships; one example is Orillas, which is a multilingual educational project concerned with language and culture. The project helps to set up relationships between sister classes in several schools throughout the United States, Canada, Puerto Rico, and Mexico and focuses on cooperative projects and activities (see References).

The Most Frightening Time in My Life

Objective

Fear is a common feeling in most children and young people's lives. Adults may consider a child's fear unimportant or irrational, but for the child, it seems very real and may cause great anxiety. This can take the form of fear of strangers, the unknown, new situations, or bad dreams. Some children's fears prevent them from learning.

During the month of October, around Halloween and All Souls' Day—"Dia de los Muertos"), children deal with their fears in a variety of ways. At school they read scary stories and create artistic ghosts and ghouls. They put on costumes with the hope of scaring others, and they talk about death and play with images such as skeletons, witches, ghosts, and monsters. During this time, children often cling more closely to their parents for safety and for the reassurance that what is happening is just pretend. When parents take the time to share recollections of some of the frightening times they have experienced in their own lives, children become more aware of fear as an acceptable human emotion. Children are able to recognize an honest expression of feelings and vulnerability, which can strengthen the bond to the parent or adult who has revealed his own fears.

Ultimately, children also succeed in looking at some fears with a sense of humor and using their fears as a creative point of departure. Sharing fears not only with one's peers, but also with adults helps to create a spirit of power and support in a group. Sometimes by changing the way we think, we can eliminate some of the fears that immobilize us.

Process

1. Begin with a discussion of some of the popular scary images or themes that the children encounter during the month of October: on the street, in the stores, at school, or on television.
2. Ask the students to share their own fears. Make a list of the fears that students have expressed.
3. Notice if particular fears are more common among class members and graph their relative popularity.
4. Have a discussion about possible ways children have dealt with these fears when they come up and about new ideas for dealing with them in the future. Do they believe these are real and justified fears, or do they believe some new knowledge could help these fears to go away?
5. Ask them what they believe their own parents or other adults they know are afraid of.
6. Try to experiment with the word "spirit" and ask the children what they would like to say to the spirit if a spirit returned to visit them one night. To whom might the spirit belong, and what would the spirit have to say to them?
7. Have the students take a letter home to their parents asking them to share the scariest incident they can recall from their childhood. You may explain to the parents that the students have been expressing some of their fears which are common around this time of the year and that it would help them to know that their own parents also had things happen to them. Let them know that you would appreciate an illustration and that you will be compiling their experiences into a book called "When We Were Young We Were Scared Too." This book will be combined with the students' writings and illustrations.

Suggestions and Reflections

My experience has been that parents really enjoy doing this activity. Most adults will find time to share these experiences with their children. Perhaps when adults return to those moments of childhood, remembering how scared they were and then realizing how much they have changed in becoming an adult, a sense of growth is promoted. It also allows the parent to give extra nurturing to the child while assuring him that he too will outgrow his fears. When compiled into a book, these memories from home produce a piece for the classroom library which the students will want to pull out time and time again. The students will also become aware that the specific country or community in which a parent grew up influences the nature of the fears. Some of these fears are connected with strong cultural and family traditions. To be continually reminded that "our parents used to be afraid too" validates the students' own fears and reassures them that they too will outgrow their fears.

A Book for Peace

Objective

The goal of this book is to find words or short phrases that concretize the feeling and idea of peace. Students take the opportunity to visualize what peace means for them. Many of their ideas will easily lend themselves to illustration. Students will be able to understand that peace is something we can all feel and create in our lives. Once again, to encourage students to express their own relationship to this concept will allow them to carry these concepts into a broader framework—hopefully into global dimensions. This book may be divided into two sections, the first written by the students and the second by the parents.

Process

1. Begin by leading a group discussion about what peace means to each of us personally. This discussion may be followed by talking about what it means to have "peace in your home," for nations to be "at peace with one another," and to have a "world at peace." What is "peaceful coexistence"?
2. Ask the students to choose one word that represents peace to them and to illustrate it as a page for the book.
3. Invite parents to send in their word or phrase and ask them to illustrate it themselves or to have their own child illustrate it for them.
4. Add the group book to the class library and share it with other classes.

Suggestions and Reflections

This book may be extremely appropriate around the winter holiday season when the words "Peace on Earth and Goodwill toward All" are commonly heard. Such phrases may be meaningless for students unless they are given some time to talk about and work with the concept. In a first-grade classroom in which this book was made, some of the students' responses were, "taking a bath," "reading," and "riding on my bike." When the parents' words came back, they included words like "reconciliation" and "communication." This provided the opportunity to explore the meanings of these new words and to enrich the children's understanding.

With older students, you may want to learn about the many areas of the world that are not at peace and try to explore and understand what the existing problems are. The concept of conflict resolution can be introduced to involve students in related classroom activities.

Find out about local and national organizations working for world peace. Think about writing letters to congressmen letting them know why peace is important to the students. Think about what you can do in your classroom to encourage peaceful interactions and work out problems in a constructive manner. You may begin to feel that a book about friendship and a book about peace have many ideas in common. Feel free to combine the two. Integrating ideas and activities always makes a stronger impact when students are engaged in learning.

part 5

EXEMPLARY PROGRAMS FOR BUILDING COMMUNITIES OF LEARNERS

chapter 11

Exemplary Programs for Building Communities of Learners

During the course of my research for this book, several programs and projects have surfaced that do not accept the deficit hypothesis of the family and community. They have created spaces for transformative possibilities. In these programs, students and their families are not merely acquiring important skills but are realizing their own worth and potential power to change their own lives and the life and future of their community. The successes of other educators can inspire us to attempt what we sometimes think would not be possible.

Some of these programs have been initiated by the families themselves; others have been launched in schools by educational consultants or researchers through grant monies; and still others have been started by a small group of teachers or even a single teacher with vision. More and more, as teachers are recognizing the need and desirability of engaging in this kind of collaborative work, they are not waiting for their districts to initiate the projects. They are seeking funding or beginning a project by donating their own time.

THE PAJARO VALLEY EXPERIENCE

The Pajaro Valley Experience in Watsonville, California (Ada, 1988), was a major successful effort to make education responsive to the needs of ethnic and linguistic minority students and their families. The project brought families together by using children's literature in Spanish as a tool to encourage discussion about parental aspirations, concerns, and values. As parents began to analyze and reflect critically on their own experiences, in relation to children's literature, they saw greater possibilities for action to effect change in both their children's schooling and lives.

The program was developed under the auspices of the Bilingual Program of the Pajaro Unified School District, which serves a mostly rural population in the area surrounding Watsonville. Fifty-four percent of the children speak Spanish, and 26 percent are from families of Mexican agricultural origins. Many of the parents have had very little schooling. Ada, a children's author and educator (1988), describes her motivations for initiating the program as part of a "decision to help parents to recover their sense of dignity and self-identity." Based on years of experience, she knew the importance of involving parents in their children's education and the essential responsibility they bear with regard to their children's future.

To begin, Ada worked with the students in classrooms and inspired their interest in literature. She initiated the parent component in order to develop greater interaction between parents and children and between parents and school.

A typical parent session is held at the public library or in the school itself for two hours on a weekday evening. During this time, the children are involved in their own program, which might consist of a story hour, a puppet show, art activities or a sing-along with a local musician. At the parents' meeting, Ada begins by leading a discussion about some area of concern or interest to the parents, such as alternatives to television or sibling rivalry. Parents then break up into small groups, with a facilitator for each group. The first task is the reading and discussion of a children's book about a topic close to the parent's reality. The participants' words and opinions become the text of a parent-authored book.

Books are created from titles such as "From Yesterday to Today," "Ourselves," "Good and Bad Things in My Life," and "Our Dreams for Our Children's Future." As each parent contributes his or her thoughts, the facilitator records them on a large wall chart. After the meeting, the words are transcribed and later copied and redistributed in the form of a book for all who were present at the meeting to read, reflect on, and enjoy.

While the parents are reading the children's literature selection, each parent holds a copy of the book as the facilitator demonstrates Ada's

(1990) "creative reading process." This strategy encourages readers to interact with a text in a very personal way. They are encouraged to make connections from their own life experience with the text. Participants talk about questions of fairness and justice in the book and think about ways in which their own lives may be changed or bettered. The process includes (1) the descriptive phase, (2) the personal/interactive phase, (3) the critical/multicultural phase, and (4) the creative or transformative phase. Parents are invited to take the books home and to share them with their children in a similar fashion as experienced in the parent session. Multiple copies of each book are purchased through grant monies for this purpose.

As parents become inspired by the books and by the family interactions around children's literature, many begin to write their own stories at home. At each session, blank books are provided for writing and illustrating at home, and each new session begins with a celebration of the authors. Families also write and read their own poetry.

For Ada (1988), the integrated person is seen as the subject or "protagonist" of his own life or story. In the telling or writing of that story, he recognizes himself as the central character instead of a secondary one. He creates his own reality through the creation of his own story. Ada's philosophy as exemplified in this program has strongly motivated the work presented in the book.

PROJECTO LIBRE

In Oceanside, California, Cristina Valdez has initiated Projecto Libre, a family literacy program based on Ada's work in Pajaro Valley and Goldsmith and Handel's work in New York City (1989). Valdez received a Title VII Federal Grant for a three-year project; these grant monies provide services for families who are learning English. This program included an ESL (English as a Second Language) component for the parents.

Spanish bilingual teachers at the school site were recruited and participated in an initial training, which included an exploration and self-education based on readings of the philosophies of Freire, Auerbach, and Poplin. These works were discussed in group sessions. Direct strategies for the program were adopted from the work of Ada and Goldsmith. Although all the teachers were excited by the concepts, many were surprised at how much extra time and work the project required. The grant paid them for the time.

The program takes place twice weekly and is divided into two parts. During the first hour, families work together in the creation of books. Different genres from the California State Literature Framework are explored, which provide the motivation and model for the families' creation of their own books. Many "Big Books" are included, while the teacher guides the participants in a discussion that relates the literature being read to connections with their own lives. The genres include fables, poetry, story telling, oral traditions, fiction, and nonfiction.

During the second part, parents and students divide themselves into two groups. The parents participate in a meaning-based ESL instruction program, whereas their children engage in activities based on hands-on art, science, and literacy. Many of the ideas that inspire this kind of liberatory ESL practice are discussed in the work of Auerbach and Wallerstein (1987) and Freire (1973). Teachers read and discuss this work in their preparatory sessions. Once a month this group of parents, and many others, come together to discuss topics of common concern, which include drugs, gangs, and helping children with homework. As parents begin to take the opportunity to discuss issues of importance to them and also become participants in a learning process that is based on experiential knowledge, feelings of self-efficacy and personal empowerment begin to grow.

THE FOUNDATION CENTER FOR PHENOMENOLOGICAL RESEARCH, INC.

This type of parent empowerment is also growing and is developing through work being done at the Foundation Center for Phenomenological Research, Inc., based in Sacramento, California, under the direction of Antonia Lopez. The foundation administers eighteen Montessori preschools and thirty family daycare homes in nine California counties. The centers believe that the child learns best within the context of his or her family and community; thus, the involvement of both is of primary importance in the education of the children. The Montessori environment is an extension or addition to the home, not a replacement for it. The model builds on the child's home and community and supports the parent's role and responsibility as the ultimate teacher and influence on the child's growth and development. Lopez (1988) asserts that schools need to adopt curricula that are "philosophically consistent" with community goals.

Educator and researcher Lily Wong-Fillmore (1990) praises the work of the centers and views the teachers as "cultural and linguistic bridges." In fact, the teachers are recruited from the homes and communities of the children, and trained to be teachers through the center's program. Their responsibility is to connect the world of the home and the school by building on what the children have learned at home as a basis for further learning. The families are the lifeblood of the centers, rather than being pushed aside or looked upon as irrelevant (p. 5). Lopez (1990) has discovered that the Montessori philosophy has helped to break down the walls that have existed between the schools and the Latino communities.

Heath's research findings (1986) appear to corroborate the conclusions reached by the centers. She asserts that most linguistic minority groups are not willing to accept parent education from those outside their community. The rearing of children is really a private or community responsibility. Few groups will allow noncommunity members to raise their young or will accept their advice on how they should raise them. The impetus for change is at the heart of one's value system and needs to come from within the individual or community itself. Programs that embark on the goal of teaching parents how to prepare their children for school "linguistically" have shown a very low success rate and do not promise to bring about any "significant internal changes" in families (Heath, 1986, p. 181).

WAYS WITH WORDS

In *Ways with Words* (1983), Heath worked with two working-class black and white communities in the Piedmont region of the Carolinas in an effort to find out how children learn to use language in their homes and communities. Teachers were able to bring the children's "ways with words" into their classroom. They discovered that the way children related to the printed word was embedded in their daily life experiences. Meaning was not derived through the learning of isolated pieces of information or individual letters, but through real messages that were usually surrounded by oral communication.

An important part of Heath's project was to enable students to articulate how the knowledge they had already gained from their homes and communities related to what the school wanted them to know. The teachers in the project learned to pay positive attention to the students' different ways of knowing and talking and did not view their abilities as a deficit or as in need of remediation. Students were constantly encouraged to articulate what they saw as the differences in language structures and use between their familiar world and the unfamiliar world of the classroom. They became researchers into the reality of their dual language and knowledge worlds, and they gained a new sense of self-awareness as they reconstructed a social and cognitive system of meanings. Classroom ways of learning were integrated with community ways of learning. The school made no attempt to destroy or replace the language or knowledge that the students brought to school. By studying their own ways of learning, organizing information, and talking, the students were able to use this knowledge as a foundation for learning another system, that of the school.

THE MOTHER'S READING PROGRAM

The Mother's Reading Program was initiated by the American Reading Council in New York City in 1984. Arrastia (1991) describes the program. The council's support for the program was based on the belief that "in order to break through the wall of illiteracy, teaching reading must be an intergenerational activity" (Barbara Bush Foundation, 1989, p. 32). The council proposed to demonstrate that teaching reading to both mothers and children in the same environment and through the same techniques would pave the way to true literacy. They became aware that participants needed to feel a deep sense of usefulness for literacy and literature in order to integrate them into their daily lives. In this program, children attend the Head Start program and are involved in oral language and story-telling activities. Children dictate stories to teachers, who listen and write them down.

During the same time, the mothers attend literacy classes where, as a group and through dialogue they create literature about the concerns in their own lives and the life of their community. This community literature becomes the core text for their reading as well as the tool to build language skills. A lending library for adults and children is an important component of the program and is used extensively by the families. This is another example of making literacy socially significant rather than a burdensome chore.

THE INTERGENERATIONAL MODEL OF EMPOWERMENT

Goldsmith and Handel (1989), instructors of adult basic education, have created an intergenerational reading program in which children's literature is also used. The adult students are introduced to stimulating and provocative books that they take home and use to re-create a literary experience with children. The instructors believe that if students are addressed in their roles as parents, as competent adults rather than as deficient readers, then their own new learning processes will begin to build on the strengths they possess within these roles.

Goldsmith and Handel's model consists of a series of participatory workshops that target a specific genre of children's literature. Through discussion and writing, students relate the literature to their personal experiences and begin to use good reading strategies, such as making predictions, to analyze the literature and improve their own reading skills. "By casting students in a proactive role, both in the instructional setting and in reading to children, the intergenerational model is one of empowerment" (p. 27).

Many educators are beginning to discover that, by focusing on the real concerns of their students, they can help to make literacy socially significant in the family's life rather than a burden. In this way, too, they can acknowledge and invite the student's reality into the classroom as an integral component of the text for learning.

All the programs I have discussed share a respect for the participants and place considerable value on participant knowledge, intelligence, and ability as a lifelong learner. Learning about each program adds a new perspective to our work, a tool for expanding on what we are already doing, or a seed to initiate a new direction within the context of our own current work.

Conclusion

Throughout this book I have tried to show that the parents' clearest connection to the school and their children's education is the classroom and the classroom teacher. If teachers welcome and validate parents by listening to their concerns and finding positive things to communicate to them about their children's ongoing progress, then the parents will most likely be open to a partnership. The teacher's words will be received with an open heart and mind. On the other hand, if teachers believe that parents don't care or are too tired or apathetic to be interested in their children's education, then the parents will be likely to fulfill those negative expectations.

Most parents appreciate and initially need a direct connection to their child's schooling through the classroom. The teacher provides the bridge from school to home. Parents want to be able to voice their concerns and aspirations, in a comfortable setting, to someone they know cares about them and their children. They value someone who respects them as parents and as the first teachers of their children. They also appreciate someone who is interested in their home culture and takes the initiative to incorporate this culture into the classroom program. They prefer to communicate with a teacher who speaks and understands their language because they want to receive input from the school that they can understand. In short, they want to feel that they are contributing to their children's education.

For their part, teachers need to understand that the relationship they establish with parents is important, ultimately holding the power to alienate the family and therefore sever the connection between home and school. Because not all teachers are comfortable with parents or with authentic communication, the development of this sensitivity and skill needs to be addressed in both teacher education programs and ongoing faculty sessions. A true partnership between home and school will not be possible until all parties, especially teachers and administrators, commit themselves to transcending the prescribed roles and behaviors.

For example, participants in my first grade study stated that homework was a clear way that parents could involve themselves with their children's education. Looking back on my own years of teaching, I now realize that I had underestimated its importance and did not listen to the parents' perspective. Today I believe that the issue of homework needs to be carefully reconsidered as one way to begin building bridges that can involve the whole family in literacy development. Homework can be meaningful to the entire family and something they can enjoy doing together. It could become a vital aspect of school life, helping to create a partnership with parents and students that will nurture literacy and facilitate participation in the schools while celebrating and validating the home culture and family concerns and aspirations.

Initially the process of co-authorship of books needs to be presented to parents in small group sessions and nurtured to a point where families can achieve a comfortable independence with the process. Because not all the households represented within the classroom are financially equal, all families should receive material support such as the boxes of materials that were presented to each participant in the first-grade project discussed in Chapter 6. In addition, celebrations in which family authors are recognized are important in supporting the process.

Based both on a review of the literature on family education and the knowledge I have gained in preparing this book, it is clear that this kind of work must be placed within the context of transformative education. Educators can no longer uncritically accept the reality that claims that there is not enough time or money to confront real issues. Educators must embrace a "public mission of making society more democratic. True democracy is a celebration of difference. Educators must speak in the language of possibility that goes beyond critique to elaborate a positive language of human empowerment" (Giroux, 1988a, pp. 95, 96).

The relationship between schools and society holds primary importance today. The priority of the present U.S. government, as demonstrated by its financial allocations, is clearly not education. Educators need to engage in an active challenge to the existing power structures which continue to promote the status quo whereby only some students are given access to a full education.

The school must be a welcoming and validating experience in the lives of young students and their families, and it must become an integral part of community life. As a first priority, relationships that will nurture trust and understanding between the classroom teacher and the student and family must be developed. This implies a redefinition of roles. That is, the teacher will no longer be in the sole position of power, serving as the only person with important knowledge deserving of respect

(Cummins, 1986). Moreover, parents need to be seen as equal contributors of knowledge and understanding to the educative process, especially in relation to their own children, community, and culture. The students' cultural diversity and the families' lived experience need to become part of the school, but most importantly, they must become part of the classroom learning environment and the development of the curriculum.

School personnel can no longer attempt to educate children in a vacuum, divorcing them from the reality of their lives and denying their parents' full input and participation. With so few successes to their credit, urban public schools can no longer afford to look at the home as a "deficit" environment or claim that "illiteracy is hereditary" and that parents "just don't care." Parents do care and they want to be involved.

Afterword

One of the most important insights articulated in *Building Communities of Learners* and demonstrated in the practice author Sudia Paloma McCaleb describes is that educators are *not* powerless to change the "realities" of their working environments or the learning environments of the students they teach. While increasing cultural and linguistic diversity in schools has presented formidable challenges to educators regardless of their ideological persuasions, it has also expanded dramatically the scope of what can be achieved through education. The monocultural chauvinism that has characterized educational systems throughout the world since the beginnings of universal formal education is highly counterproductive in an era in which economic, cultural, scientific, and existential interdependence between nations is the norm. Educating students for global citizenship is the inescapable obligation of educators engaged in preparing their students for life in the twenty-first century. The potential to achieve this goal is obviously greater in a classroom context where cultural diversity truly thrives than in a classroom context where cultural diversity is either excluded or suppressed.

At a superficial level there is general agreement among U.S. educators and policy-makers that schools should take account of the trends toward globalization in their curricula and pedagogy. For example, there have been sporadic calls for more effective foreign language teaching during the past twenty years, and multicultural education is tolerated so long as it remains at the innocuous level of acknowledging variety in food, costume, and celebrations. However, this acknowledgment of the need to learn about the "other" is merely apparent. It is undermined by the simultaneous insistence that foreign languages be taught by methods that have demonstrated their ineffectiveness for the vast majority of students, and by the absolute rejection of forms of multicultural education

195

that might challenge either the cultural myopia of the dominant group or the power structure in the society (e.g., as articulated powerfully by Nieto, 1992).

During the Reagan/Bush years, a variety of neoconservative academics (e.g., Hirsch, 1987; Porter, 1990; Schlesinger, 1991) articulated a form of intellectualized xenophobia intended to alert the general public to the infiltration of the "other" into the heart and soul of American institutions. Cultural diversity became the enemy within, far more potent and insidious in its threat than any external enemy. Hirsch's "cultural literacy" represented a call to strengthen the national immune system so that it could successfully resist the debilitating influence of cultural diversity. Only when the national identity has been fortified and secured through "cultural literacy" should contact with the "other" be contemplated, and even then educators should keep diversity at a distance, always vigilant against its potent destructive power.

It is in this context that we can understand statements such as the following from Arthur Schlesinger, Jr. (1991) in his book *The Disuniting of America*:

> In recent years the combination of the ethnicity cult with a flood of immigration from Spanish-speaking countries has given bilingualism new impetus. . . . Alas, bilingualism has not worked out as planned: rather the contrary. Testimony is mixed, but indications are that bilingual education retards rather than expedites the movement of Hispanic children into the English-speaking world and that it promotes segregation rather than it does integration. Bilingualism shuts doors. It nourishes self-ghettoization, and ghettoization nourishes racial antagonism. . . . Using some language other than English dooms people to second-class citizenship in American society. . . . Monolingual education opens doors to the larger world. . . . Institutionalized bilingualism remains another source of the fragmentation of America, another threat to the dream of 'one people' (1991, pp. 108–109).

The claims that "bilingualism shuts doors" and "monolingual education opens doors to the wider world" are laughable if viewed in isolation, particularly in the context of current global interdependence. They become interpretable only in the context of a societal discourse that is profoundly disquieted by the fact that the sounds of the "other" have now become audible and the hues of the American social landscape have darkened noticeably. Demographic projections of increasing diversity, particularly the rapid growth in the Spanish-speaking population, generate tremors presaging dramatic shifts in the structure of power within the nation.

This discourse is broadcast through the media into every classroom in the nation. There is anger that schools have apparently reneged on their traditional duty to render the "other" invisible and inaudible. Under the guise of equity programs initiated in the 1960s, diversity infiltrated into the American classroom and became legitimated by those who, in Tom Bethell's phrase, "never did think that another idea, the United States of America, was a particularly good one to begin with, and that the sooner it is restored to its component 'ethnic' parts the better off we shall all be" (1979, p. 30). There is currently immense pressure on teachers and administrators to abandon initiatives like bilingual education and multicultural education and revert to traditional forms of indoctrination that allegedly served the nation well for more than 200 years.

It is within this pattern of discourse that the theory and practice described by Sudia Paloma McCaleb should be interpreted. The preceding pages of this book strongly repudiate the racism and xenophobia advocated by neoconservative commentators and their media acolytes. The establishment of genuine partnerships between culturally diverse parents and teachers challenges the ways in which diversity has been defined as a threat by the dominant group and illustrates the creative potential that can be unleashed when coercive relations of power are replaced by collaborative relations that generate mutual empowerment. Almost by definition, establishment of collaborative relations of power between schools and communities constitutes a challenge to the societal power structure. The coercive process of defining the "other" as inferior to legitimate the other's physical and/or psychological confinement (e.g., in special education classes) is exposed and refuted by the ways in which academic and personal power are generated within the home and school partnerships described in this book.

The experiences described here also challenge the dominant group discourse that concerns "parental involvement." Despite the fact that the term lines the pages of the many manuals of school effectiveness that have been produced during the past twenty years, one can search in vain in most of this literature to find examples of genuine partnership between schools and parents from culturally diverse backgrounds. Because parents fail to show up to meetings designed to teach them "parenting skills" or other strategies for overcoming their children's "deficits," educators assume that they are just not interested in their children's education and that this clearly contributes to children's massive rates of educational failure. Lloyd Dunn (1987), the author of the widely used Peabody Picture Vocabulary Test, explicitly blames Latino parents for their children's academic difficulties when he argues that "teachers are not miracle workers" (p. 65) and "Hispanic pupils and their parents have also failed the schools and society, because they have not been motivated and dedicated enough to make the system work for them" (p. 78). In short, educators are powerless to reverse the debilitating effects of apathetic and incompetent Latino parents (whom Dunn also regards as genetically inferior [p. 64]).

The twin discourses of cultural diversity representing the enemy within and culturally diverse parents being disinterested in their children's education give rise to self-fulfilling forms of interaction in schools wherein students' experiences are systematically excluded from instruction and their identities devalued. These discourses combine to legitimate organizational structures in schools (e.g., English-only instruction) and forms of role definition or mind-sets on the part of educators that make education a punitive experience for students. Educational success requires alienation from self and community, as illustrated in Richard Rodriguez' (1982) poignant account of his childhood. The oppositional behaviors that students adopt to resist the devaluation of their identities frequently contribute to academic failure (Fordham, 1990).

Sudia Paloma McCaleb's account of her own practice and of other recent examples (e.g. Ada, 1988) exposes the coercive intent of these neoconservative discourses. Parents who have survived brutal oppression in their home countries and are experiencing poverty and hardship as they struggle to raise their children care passionately about their children's education. However, if ability to speak English and knowledge of North American cultural conventions are made prerequisites for "parental involvement," then many of these parents will be defined as apathetic and incompetent, as illustrated by Dunn's (1987) diatribe against Latino parents. Within the interactional space created by certain forms of school organization and educator role definitions, these parents will play out their preordained role of "uninvolvement." These interactional spaces between educators and communities reflect the coercive relations of power operating in the broader society between dominant and subordinated groups.

This is a dangerous book because it exposes the structures of disempowerment that masquerade as "normal" patterns of interaction between schools and culturally diverse communities. Furthermore, unlike much of the literature in the area of critical pedagogy, this book challenges coercive relations of power not by abstract theoretical analyses but through the eloquence of a mutually empowering practice that creates interactional spaces within which students, parents, and teachers can grow together. Sudia Paloma McCaleb has shown that many of the "realities" of schooling are socially constructed—part of a coercive definitional process designed to disempower—and are thus capable of being deconstructed through the collaborative action of teachers, parents, and students working together. For the countless numbers of educators striving to promote dignity and academic equity for their students, she has provided access to concrete pedagogical strategies that are profound in their social and political implications.

Jim Cummins
Ontario Institute for Studies in Education

References for the Afterword

Ada, A. F. (1988). The Pajaro Valley experience. Working with Spanish-speaking parents to develop children's reading and writing skills in the home through the use of children's literature. In T. Skutnabb-Kangas & J. Cummins (Eds.), *Minority education: From shame to struggle* (pp. 223–238). Clevedon, England: Multilingual Matters.

Bethell, T. (1979, February). Against bilingual education: why Johnny can't speak English. *Harper's*, 30–33.

Dunn, L. (1987). *Bilingual Hispanic children on the U.S. mainland: A review of research on their cognitive, linguistic, and scholastic development.* Circle Pines, Minnesota: American Guidance Service.

Fordham, S. (1990). Racelessness as a factor in Black students' school success: Pragmatic strategy or pyrrhic victory? In N. M. Hidalgo, C. L. McDowell, and E. V. Siddle (Eds.), *Facing racism in education* (pp. 232–262). Reprint series No. 21, Harvard Education Review.

Hirsch, E. D., Jr. (1987). *Cultural literacy: What every American needs to know.* Boston: Houghton Mifflin.

Nieto, S. (1992). *Affirming diversity: The sociopolitical context of multicultural education.* New York: Longman.

Porter, R. P. (1990). *Forked tongue: The politics of bilingual education.* New York: Basic Books.

Rodriguez, R. (1982). *Hunger of memory: The education of Richard Rodriguez.* Boston: David R. Godine.

Schlesinger, A., Jr. (1991). *The disuniting of America.* New York: W. W. Norton.

References

Ada, A. F. (1988). The Pajaro Valley experience: Working with Spanish-speaking parents to develop children's reading and writing skills in the home through the use of children's literature. In T. Skutnabb-Kangas & J. Cummins (Eds.), *Minority education: From shame to struggle* (pp. 223-238). Philadelphia: Multi-Lingual Matters.

Ada, A. F. (1990). *A magical encounter.* Compton, Calif.: Santillana Publishing.

Ada, A. F. (1993, March/April). CABE '93 a resounding success: World-renowned educator Paulo Freire inspires opening general session. *CABE Newsletter*, 1, 25.

Ada, A. F., & Beutel, C. (1991). "Participatory research as dialogue for action." Unpublished manuscript, University of San Francisco.

Arrastia, M. (1991). Community literature in the multicultural classroom: The mother's reading program. In C. Walsh (Ed.), *Literacy as praxis: Culture, language and pedagogy.* Northwood, N.J.: Ablex Publishing Corp.

Ashton-Warner, S. (1969). *Teacher.* New York: Simon & Schuster.

Auerbach, E. (1990). *Making meaning, making change.* Boston: University of Massachusetts.

Auerbach, E., & Wallerstein, N. (1987). *English for the workplace: ESL in action, problem posing at work.* New York: Addison-Wesley Publishing.

Barbara Bush Foundation for Family Literacy. (1989). *First teachers: A family literacy handbook for parents, policy makers, and literacy providers.* Washington, D.C.: Author.

Becher, R. S. (1986). Parent involvement: A review of research and principles of successful practice. In L. G. Katz (Ed.), *Current topics in early childhood education.* Vol. VI. Norwood, N.J.: Ablex.

Belenky, M. F., et al. (1986). *Women's ways of knowing: The development of self, voice, and mind.* New York: Basic Books.

Black, K. (Singer and Composer). (1991). *Ya Gotta Know Something 'Bout History*. Berkeley, Calif.: Heebie Jeebie Music.

Brim, O. G. (1959). *Education for child rearing*. New York: Russell Sage Foundation.

Chall, J. S., & Snow, C. (1982). *Families and literacy: The contributions of out of school experiences to children's acquisition of literacy: A final report to the National Institute of Education*. Cambridge, Mass.: Harvard Families and Literacy Project.

Clark, R. M. (1983). *Family life and school achievement*. Chicago: University of Chicago Press.

Cummins, J. (1981). The role of primary language development in promoting educational success for language minority students. In *Schools and Language Minority Students: A theoretical framework*. Los Angeles: California State University.

Cummins, J. (1986). Empowering minority students: A framework for intervention. *Harvard Educational Review* 56, 18-34.

Cummins, J. (1989). *Empowering minority students*. Sacramento, Calif.: California Association for Bilingual Education.

Darder, A. (1991). *Culture and power in the classroom: A critical foundation for bicultural education*. New York: Bergin & Garvey.

Delgado-Gaitan, C. (1987). Mexican adult literacy: New directions for immigrants. In S. R. Goldman & K. Trueba (Eds.), *Becoming literate in English as a second language*. Norwood, N.J.: Ablex.

Delpit, L. (1988). The silenced dialogue: Power and pedagogy in educating other people's children. *Harvard Educational Review* 58(3), 280-298.

Dewey, J. (1938). *Experience and education*. New York: Macmillan Publishing Co.

Diaz, S., Moll, L., & Mehan, H. (1986). Socio-cultural resources in instruction: A context-specific approach. In *Beyond language: Social and cultural factors in schooling language minority children*. Los Angeles: California State Department of Education and California State University.

Edelsky, C., Altwerger, B., & Flores, B. (1991). *Whole language: What's the difference?* Portsmouth, N.H.: Heinemann Educational Books.

Figueroa, Ed., Sayers, D., and Brown, K. (1991). *De Orilla a Orilla—Una red multilingue e intercultural para el aprendizaje cooperativo*. Pamphlet.

Freire, P. (1970). *Pedagogy of the oppressed*. New York: Continuum.

Freire, P. (1973). *Education for critical consciousness*. New York: Seabury Press.

Gilligan, C. (1982). *In a Different Voice*. Cambridge, Mass.: Harvard University Press.

Giroux, H. (1983). *Theory and Resistance in Education: A Pedagogy for the Opposition*. New York: Bergin and Garvey.

Giroux, H. (1988a). The hope of radical education: A conversation with Henry Giroux. *Journal of Education*, 170, 91-101.

Giroux, H. (1988b). *Schooling and the struggle for public life.* Minneapolis: University of Minnesota Press.

Giroux, H. (1989). Rethinking education reforms in the age of George Bush. *Phi Delta Kappan, 70,* 728-730.

Giroux, H. (1990a, March/April). A pedagogy for democracy. *CABE Newsletter, 12,* 16.

Giroux, H. (1990b, January). Keynote speech at the annual Conference of the California Association of Bilingual Education. San Francisco.

Goldenberg, C. N. (1984). Low income parents' contributions to reading achievement of their first grade children. Paper presented at the meeting of the Evaluation Network/Evaluation Research Society (Oct. 10-13), San Francisco.

Goldsmith, E., & Handel, R. (1989). Children's literature and adult literacy: Empowerment through intergenerational learning. *Lifelong Learning, 12* (6), 24-27.

Goodman, K. (1992). I didn't found whole language. *The Reading Teacher, 46,* 188-199.

Goodson, B. D., Millsap, M., & Swartz, J. (1991). *Working with families: Promising programs to help parents support young children's learning.* Final report for U.S. Department of Education, Office of Planning, Budget and Evaluation (Contract No. LC 8808901). Cambridge, Mass.: Abt Associates Inc.

Greenspan, R., Niemeyer, J. H., & Seeley, D. (1991). *Principals speak: Report #1: Restructuring schools and school leadership.* New York: Research Foundation of City University of New York.

Greenspan, R., Niemeyer, J. H., & Seeley, D. (1991). *Principals speak: Report #2: Parent involvement.* New York: Research Foundation of City University of New York.

Heath, S. B. (1983). *Ways with words.* Cambridge: Cambridge University Press.

Heath, S. B. (1986). Sociocultural contexts of language development. In *Beyond language: Social and cultural factors in schooling language minority children.* Los Angeles: California State Department of Education and California State University.

Hirsch, E. D. (1987). *Cultural Literacy: What every American needs to know.* Boston: Houghton Mifflin.

hooks, b. (1989). *Talking back, thinking feminist, thinking black.* Boston: South End Press.

Horton, M., & Freire, P. (1991). *We make the road by walking.* Philadelphia: Temple University Press.

Institute for Education in Transformation. (1992). *Voices from the inside: A report on schooling from inside the classroom.* Claremont, Calif.: Claremont Graduate School.

Institute for Innovations in Social Policy. (1991). *1991 index of social health: Monitoring the social well-being of the nation.* Tarrytown, N.Y.: Fordham University.

Kagan, S. (1986). Cooperative learning and socio-cultural factors in schooling. In *Beyond language: Social and cultural factors in schooling language minority students.* Los Angeles: California State Department of Education and California State University.

Karp, S. (1991, May/June). Reflections of African-American immersion schools. *Rethinking Schools*, pp. 18-19.

Kieffer, C. H. (1981). *Doing dialogic retrospection: Approaching empowerment through participatory research.* Paper presented at the International Meeting of the Society for Applied Anthropology, University of Edinburgh, Edinburgh, Scotland.

Kohl, H. (1992, Autumn). I won't learn from you. *Rethinking Schools*, 7 (1), 1, 16-19.

Kozol, J. (1991). *Savage inequalities.* New York: Random House.

Levine, D. (1992-1993, Winter). Souls or dollars. *Rethinking Schools* 7 (2), 1, 14.

Lipsky, S. (1987). Internalized racism. *Black Re-Emergence Journal.* Seattle, Wash.: Rational Island Publishers.

Lopez, A. (1988). The infant-toddler and child development center and parent education and support. Paper presented at the Workshop on Early Development of Hispanic Infants and Children: Options for Intervention to Improve School Readiness and Long-Term Academic Achievement. Sponsored by the National Resource Center for Children in Poverty, Columbia University, New York.

Lopez, A. (1990). To keep the door open . . . a conversation with Antonia Lopez. *Montessori Life* 2 (3).

Miller, J. B. (1976). *Toward a New Psychology of Women,* Boston: Beacon Press.

Nieto, S. (1992). *Affirming diversity: The socio-political context of multicultural education.* New York: Longman Publishing Group.

Office of Planning, Research and Information, San Francisco Unified School District. (1991, October 15). Personal communication.

Olsen, L., & Mullen, A. (1990). *Embracing Diversity.* San Francisco: California Tomorrow.

Park, P. (1989). *What is participatory research? A theoretical and methodological perspective.* Amherst: University of Massachusetts.

Poplin, M. (1991). The two restructuring movements: Which shall it be? Transformative or reductive. Manuscript submitted for publication.

Poplin, M. (1992). A practical theory of teaching and learning: A view from inside the transformative classroom: Lessons from a pedagogy of the feminine. Manuscript submitted for publication.

Raspberry, W. (1986, March 11). Barbara Bush's pet project. *Washington Post*, p. 13.

Rethinking Columbus: Teaching about the 500th anniversary of Columbus's arrival in America. (1991). Milwaukee, Wisc.: Rethinking Schools.

Reyes, M. (1992, Winter). Challenge venerable assumptions: Literacy instruction for linguistically different students. *Harvard Educational Review,* 62 (1), 427-438.

Rothman, R. (1992, October 21). Study confirms "fears" regarding commercial tests. *Education Week,* pp. 1, 13.

Shor, I. (1986). *Culture wars: School and society in the conservative restoration 1969-1984.* Boston: Routledge & Kegan Paul.

Singleton, J. (director and writer). (1991). *Boyz N the hood.* [Film]. Burbank, Calif.: Columbia Tri Star Home Video.

Skutnabb-Kangas, T., & Cummins, J., eds. (1988). *Minority education: From shame to struggle.* Philadelphia: Multi-Lingual Matters.

Spatz, L. (1993). Personal communication. Berkeley, Calif.

Staff, *NABE News.* (1992, November 15). Census reports significant increase in language-minority population. *NABE News,* 14.

Taylor, D. (1983). *Family literacy: Young children learning to read and write.* Portsmouth, N.H.: Heinemann.

Taylor, D., & Dorsey-Gaines, C. (1988). *Growing up literate: Learning from inner-city families.* Portsmouth, N.H.: Heinemann.

Tizard, J., Schofield, W. N., & Hewison, J. (1982). Symposium: Reading collaboration between teachers and parents in assisting children's reading. *British Journal of Educational Psychology,* 52, 1-15.

Viola, M., Gray, A. J., & Murphy, B. (1986). Report on the Navajo parent-child reading program at the Chinle Primary School, Chinle School District, AZ.

Waggoner, D. (1992). Four in five home speakers of non-English languages in the United States speak one of 8 languages. *Numbers and needs: Ethnic and linguistic minorities in the United States,* 2 (5).

Walsh, C. (1991a). *Pedagogy and the struggle for voice: Issues of language, power and schooling for Puerto Ricans.* South Hadley, Mass.: Bergin & Garvey.

Walsh, C. (1991b). *Literacy as praxis: Culture, language, and pedagogy.* Northwood, N.J.: Ablex.

Wong-Fillmore, L. (1983). The language learner as an individual: Implications of research on individual differences for the ESL teacher. In M. A. Clarke & J. Handscombe, (Eds.), *On TESOL '82: Pacific perspectives on language learning and teaching* (pp. 157-171). Washington, D.C.: TESOL.

Wong-Fillmore, L. (1990). Latino families and the schools. *California Perspectives, An Anthology from California Tomorrow,* Vol. 1, San Francisco.

INDEX